The Medicinal Garden

For all the humble backyard and balcony growers giving growing a go.

The Medicinal Garden

Caroline Parker
BHSc Western Herb Med

with illustrations by Lucy Mora

Treat, feed and soothe straight from your garden

Contents

Introduction 7

01 Plant profiles and recipes 11

02 All about your herb garden 177

Growing medicinal plants 178
Herbs in containers 180
Herbs for garden care 182
Weeds 184

03 Harvesting and drying 187

Harvesting your herbs 188
Drying your herbs 190

04 Build your herbal medicine cabinet 195

Teas and infusions 196
Herbal steam inhalation 197
Herbal posy 198
Baths 199
Foot soak 200
Wash 200
Compress 201
Poultice 202
Tincture 203
Spray 205

05 Herbal charts 206

Index 212
Acknowledgements 216

Introduction

Mounting studies show that gardening is good for us, with positive outcomes for physical wellbeing and mental health. Gardening reduces stress, lowers anxiety, decreases mental fatigue and boosts mood. Even sitting for five minutes soaking up and enjoying your garden is beneficial to your health. Growing and cooking with herbs is a fun introduction to the world of herbal medicine and a great way to become familiar with their appearance, taste and health benefits.

I'm not only interested in using herbs in traditional medicinal preparations, I'm also passionate about incorporating them into our diet. Adding a wider variety of plants to the foods we eat results in an increase in vitamins, minerals and nutrients, and improves our digestive health and wellbeing. It's surprisingly easy (and tasty) to do – give marmalade a lift with the addition of a sprig of thyme or meadowsweet flower, drizzle a cake with herbal syrup, use purple elderberries and green nettles as natural food colouring, add aromatic leaves, pretty petals and herbal dressings to your salads.

I grew up with a strong curiosity for gardening and using herbs. Mum once discovered a rather pungent crop of harvested valerian hanging upside down in a paper bag in my wardrobe. When I eventually used it to make some tea, it didn't taste all that great, even with some added peppermint leaves. But it did give me the desired outcome of a restful night's sleep. It wasn't until my late twenties that I realised that working with herbs was a thing you could do as a 'job', and off I went to study for a degree in herbal medicine.

Nowadays, I have my own medicinal garden and enjoy teaching at herbal medicine workshops, hosting foraging walks and helping out at a nearby farm growing beautiful flowers. It is here that I grow a few rows of my own herbs to use in medicinal preparations and my herbal tea blends.

Herbs can soothe and support the body and provide benefits for the skin and for the digestive, respiratory, nervous systems and more.

I've learnt that the healing properties of herbs aren't just in their medicinal compounds. It's in the sowing and growing – your hands in the dirt and the sun on your back while tending to plants and the earth. Whether it's gathering leaves and flowers for a cup of garden tea, decorating a homemade cake with dried calendula petals, or enjoying and sharing the fruits of your labour, it's all deeply nurturing for the body and mind.

Starting your herb garden doesn't need to be complicated. You don't even need a dedicated spot to grow herbs. Plant them amongst your flowers, as companion plants in your vegetable

garden, start a potted tea garden or build a herb box for the kitchen windowsill.

Local nurseries often have a good range of culinary herbs, as well as a few medicinal ones. You can purchase most medicinal herb seeds and live seedlings from specialist herb and vegetable growers online. A major benefit of planting medicinal herbs by seed is that the variety available to you is much greater than what is on hand in seedling form. It is also worth checking if your local community centre has a seed-saving bank or growing group – these groups can be a great resource for swapping seeds and seedlings, as well as providing an opportunity to chat about all things gardening.

Remember, you're not a bad gardener if you don't start everything from seed. Many of the herbs in my garden have been grown from cuttings gifted by keen gardening friends or bought on impulse at Sunday markets or the hardware store. It all adds to the herb's story. Grow just one herb, add it to your cooking or add it to your tea and you'll be well on your way to starting your own medicinal garden adventure.

This book is not intended to replace individualised professional advice on healthcare and wellbeing. Its aim is to offer a helpful guide to plant medicine, and as such it is not meant to be utilised to diagnose or treat. It is recommended that you consult your naturopathic practitioner or herbalist when seeking natural healthcare support: health runs deep, and there is no such thing as a one-size-fits-all approach. It is recommended that you consult your medical practitioner before seeking or commencing natural healthcare support.

Chapter 01

Plant profiles and recipes

Yarrow

Achillea millefolium

The antibacterial and antimicrobial properties of yarrow can help to assist with the healing of small cuts, ulcers and inflamed gums. Make a poultice from the leaves and place it over the affected area. As a cold remedy, yarrow is known to help fight infection. Drink a hot cup of yarrow, elderflower and peppermint tea to support your body through a cold. The bitter taste of yarrow can support healthy digestion and may help to ease indigestion and bloating. Crush up a leaf and rub it over exposed skin to keep flies and mosquitoes away.

- **Sow** autumn, spring
- **Aspect** full to partial sun
- **Spacing** 30–45 cm (12–18 inches)
- **Height** 60 cm (23 inches)
- **Frost & drought** drought tolerant, frost tolerant
- **Soil pH** 6.0–7.5
- **Part used** flower, leaf
- **Preparation** compress, food, tea, tincture, wash
- **Good for** digestive, respiratory, skin
- **Caution** known allergen

Sow and grow

Add yarrow seeds to fine sand to help scatter them and sow seeds at a depth of 2 mm (1/16 inch). Shoots should appear in around 2 weeks.

Yarrow readily self-seeds and is also easy to propagate by division in spring and autumn.

It likes moist, rich, well-drained soil. Plant yarrow where you don't mind it taking over, as it can end up creating a fluffy green carpet through your garden.

You can encourage abundant blooms by regularly deadheading.

Harvest

Yarrow should be ready to harvest 12–16 weeks from planting.

Harvest the flowers in summer, once the whole flower head has opened. Yarrow leaves can be harvested most of the year, but they are better quality during the growing season.

Store the dried flowers and leaves in an airtight container for up to 2 years.

Anise hyssop

Agastache foeniculum

Anise hyssop has a long tradition as a remedy for soothing coughs and colds. It helps to break down mucus, ease irritated lungs and clear blocked sinuses. Anise hyssop can help support the body through fevers. It may ease feelings of nausea and alleviate digestive complaints such as diarrhoea, bloating and flatulence. Use a wash or compress of anise hyssop to soothe and heal burns and grazes, as well as reduce the itchiness from allergic rashes. It adds a gentle, minty anise flavour to tea blends, cordials, jams and jellies.

- **Sow** autumn, spring
- **Aspect** full sun to partial shade
- **Spacing** 30–45 cm (12–14 inches)
- **Height** 90 cm (35 inches)
- **Frost & drought** drought tolerant, frost tolerant
- **Soil pH** 6.0–7.0
- **Part used** flower, leaf
- **Preparation** compress, food, steam inhalation, tea, tincture, wash
- **Good for** digestive, nervous, respiratory, skin

Sow and grow

Anise hyssop seeds like a bit of cold to germinate, so stratify them in the fridge for 3–4 weeks before planting. Sow seeds at a depth of 2 mm (1/16 inch).

Anise hyssop readily self-seeds throughout the garden. It is also easy to propagate by root division in spring and autumn. Choose young roots so you don't disturb the strong taproot of the mother plant.

It prefers a moist, well-drained soil, rich in organic matter.

Anise hyssop can become a bit straggly in the garden. Pinch off the fresh, young growing tips every week or so to encourage a lush and bushy plant. Encourage a second flush of blooms by regularly deadheading and give the whole plant a trim back after flowering. The plant will die down over winter in colder climates.

Harvest

Anise hyssop should be mature enough to harvest in 10–13 weeks.

Leaves can be harvested as you need them, although the best time is just before the plant flowers. Harvest flowers when the spike is fully open.

Store dried anise hyssop in an airtight container in a dry, dark place for 1–2 years.

Summer berry ice cream with anise

Makes 800 ml (27 fl oz)

This custard-based ice cream makes use of an abundance of summer berries and the anise hyssop adds a unique licorice, minty-flavoured twist.

Place the berries, elderberry syrup and anise hyssop in a small saucepan on medium–high heat and bring to a gentle simmer for 15 minutes. Give the berries a mash with a fork to help them break down. Remove from the heat and let cool to room temperature.

Using a stick blender, blitz the berry mixture for 30–60 seconds. Strain through a fine mesh sieve, then set aside while you prepare the custard base.

Use handheld electric beaters to beat the egg yolks and sugar together in a bowl until thick, light in colour and creamy in texture. Stir the vanilla extract through the eggs, then set aside.

Place the milk and cream in a medium saucepan over medium heat for 2–3 minutes. You don't need to boil or simmer the mixture; you are simply warming it.

With a whisk or electric beaters, slowly pour the warmed milk into the egg mixture. Whisk until smooth, then pour it back into the saucepan.

Cook the custard over medium heat for 5–8 minutes, stirring constantly until it is thick and coats the back of a spoon. (You should be able to run a finger along the spoon leaving a visible line in the custard.) Cover and cool to room temperature, then pop in the fridge to cool completely for 2–3 hours.

Stir the berry mixture through the custard then pour it into your ice cream maker. You can add another dash of elderberry syrup at this point to make the ice cream a little darker if you like.

Once the mixture is frozen, you can serve it straight away or pop it into the freezer to firm up a little more.

Serve with the extra berries, a drizzle of elderberry syrup and a scattering of anise hyssop leaves.

Store in an airtight container in the freezer for 2–3 weeks.

- 200 g (7 oz) blackberries, plus 65 g (2¼ oz) more to serve
- 125 ml (4 fl oz) elderberry syrup, plus extra to drizzle
- 30 g (1 oz) finely chopped anise hyssop, plus extra leaves and flowers, to serve
- 4 egg yolks
- 115 g (4 oz) caster sugar
- ¼ teaspoon vanilla extract
- 250 ml (8½ fl oz) full-cream (whole) milk
- 250 ml (8½ fl oz) pure cream

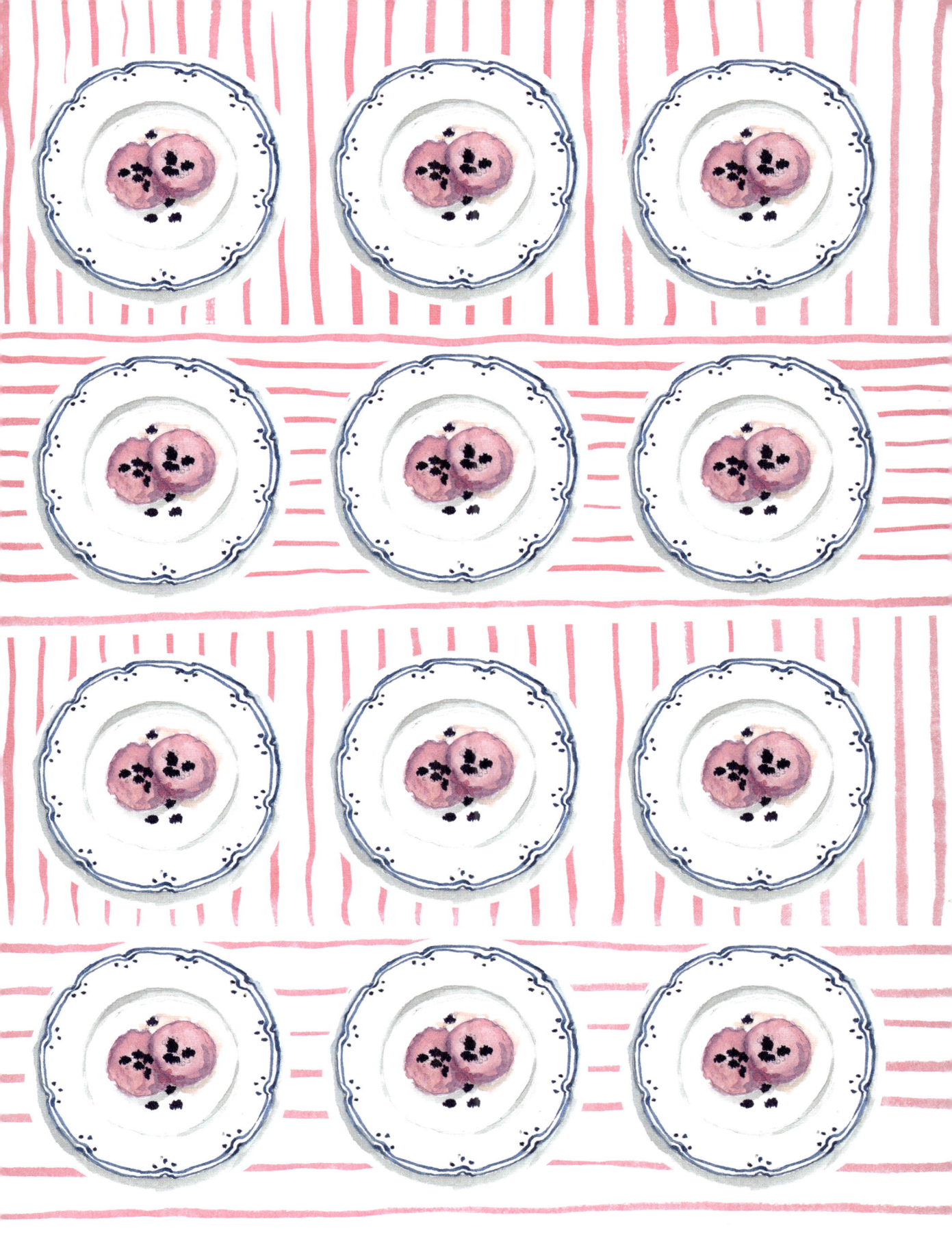

Onion

Allium cepa

The tears that spout forth when onions are chopped are a result of the presence of sulphur-containing compounds. These compounds act as decongestants, helping the body break down and expel mucus, and alleviating the symptoms of colds. Onions support healthy digestion, especially when combined with aromatic herbs like sage, thyme and oregano. They're packed with soluble fibre, which not only promotes healthy digestion but also nourishes and stimulates the growth of good gut bacteria. They can have positive effects on cardiovascular health; regulating blood pressure and maintaining healthy cholesterol levels.

- **Sow** autumn, winter
- **Aspect** full sun
- **Spacing** 10–15 cm (4–6 inches)
- **Height** 30 cm (12 inches)
- **Frost & drought** drought tolerant, frost tolerant
- **Soil pH** 6.0–7.5
- **Part used** bulb
- **Preparation** food, poultice
- **Good for** cardiovascular, digestive, respiratory
- **Caution** known allergen; avoid use alongside anticoagulant and antiplatelet drugs

Sow and grow

Onions can be grown from seeds, sets or transplants. Planting onions from seed offers a little more variety. Gently scatter the seeds on the surface of the soil. Shoots should appear in around 2 weeks.

Onions like moist, rich, well-drained soil. Mound the soil up a little to help with drainage, as onions don't like being too soggy. Keep on top of weeding and give them a monthly feed of a nitrogen-rich fertiliser to ensure big bulbs.

Harvest

Onions are ready to harvest when the stems go yellow and droop, collapsing to the ground.

Dry your onions on a well-ventilated rack for around 2 weeks before using them. If you'd like to keep them for longer, store them in a cool, dark, dry spot.

Pick and use the green stems throughout the season as a replacement for spring onions (scallions).

Dried onions will keep for up to 6 months.

Onion poultice

If you feel an ear infection coming on, try out this remedy. It may look a little silly, but it can be very effective for some people.

An onion poultice can also be used to alleviate general cold and flu symptoms.

Place the onion and 1 tablespoon of water in a frying pan and gently warm on low heat until the onion is just translucent.

Place the warmed onion on a piece of gauze, then fold it into a parcel or envelope shape. Let it cool a little so it is comfortable enough to place on your ear and not give you a burn.

Place the onion square over your ear. Use a bandage or elastic headband to help hold in place and pop your beanie over the top. Leave in place for 20 minutes.

Follow up the same treatment on your other ear, even if it's not sore. Repeat for 2–3 days.

Alternatively, place the onion poultice on the bottom of your feet and keep it in place with some woolly socks. Wear them overnight and go to bed with a hot water bottle to help reduce cold symptoms.

1 brown onion, peeled and finely chopped

10 cm (4 inch) square of gauze or cotton cloth

Garlic

Allium sativum

Garlic is a medicinal powerhouse full of plant chemicals that are antimicrobial, antibacterial, antiviral, antiseptic and antifungal. Garlic is commonly used for the treatment of colds, but it has also been shown to reduce blood pressure and cholesterol. It may also help prevent the build-up of plaque in arteries. For those on a low-FODMAP diet, you can still get the benefits from garlic by using garlic-infused oil.

- **Sow** autumn
- **Aspect** full sun
- **Spacing** 10–15 cm (4–6 inches)
- **Height** 50 cm (20 inches)
- **Frost & drought** frost and drought tolerant
- **Soil pH** 6.0–7.5
- **Part used** bulb
- **Preparation** food, infused oil, honey, tincture
- **Good for** cardiovascular, digestive, respiratory
- **Caution** known allergen; avoid using alongside anticoagulant and antiplatelet drugs

Sow and grow

Plant individual garlic cloves, pointy side up, in 5 mm (¼ inch) holes. Shoots should appear in 2–4 weeks.

Garlic likes a rich, moist, very well-drained soil. Mulch well over garlic to suppress weeds during its long growing time.

When garlic produces a rigid flower stem (scape), it is called a 'hardneck' variety. Hardneck varieties often have larger but fewer cloves per bulb than 'softneck' varieties. Hardneck varieties grow well in colder climates. Softneck varieties don't have a scape and grow well in milder climates.

In hardneck varieties, remove the scape when it starts to get curly, this will encourage bulb growth as opposed to flower growth. Use your garlic scapes in cooking anywhere that you would normally use garlic or spring onions (scallions).

Harvest

Garlic should be ready to harvest 6–9 months from planting.

When the leaves begin to yellow and wilt, you can check the size of the garlic by gently scraping away some of the soil at the top of the bulb. If it's big enough, go right ahead and dig it up, and if not, leave it in the ground to mature a little more.

Trim the scape from the bulb of hardneck varieties when harvesting and store by hanging in bunches. Lay garlic on a drying rack or hang it in a dry area for around 2 months. If you have softneck garlic, you can plait the stems and hang them.

Store dried garlic for up to 10 months in a cool, dry spot.

Fermented garlic honey

My herbalist friend Kathy downs whole cloves of raw garlic, calling them her 'cold and flu tablets'. I reckon a clove of fermented garlic honey is a much tastier option. Adding other medicinal herbs like sage, thyme and oregano will provide an extra health kick. Use a spoonful of honey in hot ginger and lemon tea easing colds and flu. Add honey into marinades and dressings, the cloves of garlic into roast dinners, and pop into a Garden greens dip (page 171).

1 bulb of garlic

glass jar with lid, big enough for the garlic

1–2 teaspoons dried herbs (optional)

raw honey, enough to cover the garlic

✱ **Caution** Honey should not be given to children under the age of one.

Peel and crush the garlic, adding it to the jar until it is three quarters full. Add a teaspoon or two of additional herbs into the jar if desired.

Fill the jar with enough honey to cover all the garlic, making sure to leave about an inch free at the top of the jar. Stir with a knife to remove any air bubbles. Weigh down the garlic under the honey with a fermenting weight and seal the jar with an airtight lid.

Let the garlic macerate in a cool, dark spot in your cupboard for 1–2 weeks. Give it a good stir and burp once a day (opening the lid to remove gas). You may need to top the jar up with honey and check that the garlic is still completely covered. The longer you leave it, the deeper the flavour.

The fermented garlic honey can be stored for up to 12 months. You can remove and use the cloves at any point during the fermentation process.

Aloe vera

Aloe barbadensis

Aloe is well known for its skin soothing and healing properties. It cools and calms inflamed skin, burns, grazes, insect bites and relieves itching. The antibacterial, antiseptic and anti-inflammatory properties of aloe make it great for oral health. It can help to treat gum disease, reduce plaque build-up and alleviate mouth ulcers. Make a mouthwash from aloe vera gel to help keep gums healthy and prevent gingivitis. Aloe can also help to balance stomach acid, look after the health of beneficial gut bacteria and aid in regulating bowel movements.

- **Sow** summer, autumn, spring
- **Aspect** full sun
- **Spacing** 30–45 cm (12–14 inches)
- **Height** 80 cm (31 inches)
- **Frost & drought** drought tolerant, frost tender
- **Soil pH** 6.0–7.0
- **Part used** gel, leaf
- **Preparation** food, topical application
- **Good for** digestive, skin
- **Caution** avoid internal use during pregnancy and lactation; use only for short periods of time

Sow and grow

Aloes are best grown from bare-rooted plants, 'pups' or cuttings. Plant them straight into the ground. Transplanted aloes can be top-heavy and will require a structure to support them while they re-establish their roots.

They like well-drained soil, but allow the soil to dry out between watering to avoid root rot.

Remove any dead leaves.

Harvest

Harvest aloes during the warmer months. Choose plants with an established root system and plenty of large, outer leaves. Don't harvest more than a third of the plant at a time and cut the leaves as close to the stem as possible.

Let the harvested leaves sit cut-side down on a dish for 5–10 minutes, until the yellow latex drains off. This part of the aloe is very bitter and can be irritating to sensitive skin and can really upset your stomach. Cut the spikes off along the sides of the leaf, then cut the leaf in half and scoop out the fleshy gel with a small teaspoon. Give the gel a good wash to help remove any residual latex.

If you are not going to use it straight away, you can pop the gel in the fridge for a few days or you can freeze it in ice cube trays. The whole leaves freeze well too.

Both the whole leaf and processed aloe will keep in the freezer for up to 6 months.

Aloe vera popsicles

Makes 480 ml (16 fl oz)

This tasty, cooling treat is great for aiding digestion and rehydrating after a busy day in the garden. You can play around with this recipe to suit your tastes. Try adding a couple of teaspoons of matcha powder or, for a summery treat, add some seasonal berries – blueberries are particularly good. Add a dash of gin or Pimm's for a grown-up treat.

Place the aloe gel and roughly chopped cucumber in a blender and blitz until smooth. Strain the mixture through a fine mesh sieve. Discard the strained pulp in the compost.

To the aloe liquid, add the lime and lemon juice, coconut water and agave nectar and whisk until well combined. Add the mint.

Pour the mixture evenly into your icy pole moulds and decorate with the thinly sliced cucumber rounds. You can pop some pretty flowers from your herb garden in too if you like.

Place in the freezer for 3–4 hours or until frozen through.

Popsicles will keep in the freezer for up to 6 months.

- 2 tablespoons aloe vera gel (equivalent 1 aloe vera leaf)
- ½ continental cucumber, roughly chopped, plus ½ more thinly sliced to decorate
- juice of 2 limes
- juice of ½ lemon
- 250 ml (8½ fl oz) coconut water
- 3 teaspoons agave nectar, maple syrup or honey
- 15 g (½ oz) mint leaves, roughly chopped
- petals or flowers from calendula, catnip, lemon balm (optional)

Marshmallow

Althaea officinalis

Marshmallow can assist in providing relief to irritated and inflamed membranes in the digestive, respiratory and urinary systems, alleviating conditions such as sore throats, dry spasmodic coughs, bronchitis, urinary tract infections and irritable bowel syndrome. It may also help to heal burns, eczema, superficial wounds and ulcers, as well as providing relief to dry, itchy skin. All parts of the marshmallow plant are edible. The leaves can be used like leafy greens in stir-fries, soups, stews, smoothies and salads. The roots can be boiled and roasted like other root vegetables and the flowers can be brewed as tea or popped into pretty salads.

- **Sow** autumn, spring
- **Aspect** full sun to partial shade
- **Spacing** 60–90 cm (23–35 inches)
- **Height** 120 cm (47 inches)
- **Frost & drought** drought tender, frost tolerant
- **Soil pH** 6.0–7.5
- **Part used** flower, leaf, root
- **Preparation** compress, food, tea, tincture, wash
- **Good for** digestive, respiratory, skin, urinary
- **Caution** may reduce absorption of prescribed drugs if taken within an hour or so of each other

Sow and grow

Scarify marshmallow seeds by rubbing between a medium grit sandpaper, then stratify in the fridge for 3–4 weeks before sowing. Scatter the seeds lightly on the surface of the soil. Shoots should appear in around 2 weeks.

Marshmallow will self-seed and is easy to propagate by division in autumn.

Marshmallow likes moist, rich, well-drained soil and regular watering. Marshmallow can be grown in pots, but it's harder to maintain the moist soil they like. If you do plant one in a pot, they'll need a big pot for their roots and to support their height.

Encourage abundant blooms by regularly deadheading. Trim your marshmallow plant back in late autumn, when the plant starts yellowing and dying down. Mulch around the crown and you will have lovely new shoots appearing in spring.

Harvest

The aerial parts of marshmallow should be ready to harvest in around 17 weeks from planting.

Harvest the leaves during the growing season as you need them. Gather the flowers in summer. The roots will take around 2 years of growth before they are mature enough to harvest. Harvest in autumn, when the plant has died down.

Be patient when drying the roots – they should be crispy when dry.

Store dried marshmallow in an airtight container for up to 2 years.

Rose, hibiscus and vanilla marshmallows

Makes 16

Homemade marshmallows have the health benefits of the herb packed into a yummy sweet treat. Use like a normal marshmallow – pop one in your hot chocolate, add it to homemade rocky road, or roast one on a stick over a winter campfire.

Grease and line a 18 x 28 cm (7 x 11 inch) brownie pan with baking paper.

Use a food processor to blitz the marshmallow root, rose petals and hibiscus to a powder. Push through a fine mesh sieve to remove any coarse particles. Pop these back in the food processor and blitz until powdery and then push through the sieve once more.

Place 310 ml (10½ fl oz) of water and the herb powder into a small saucepan and stir together on medium heat. Once simmering, turn the heat down to low to keep the liquid at a gentle simmer for 15 minutes. The liquid will reduce down. Remove from the heat and strain through a fine mesh sieve. Pour 250 ml (8½ fl oz) of the liquid into another small saucepan and add the gelatine powder. Whisk together over low heat for around 5 minutes, or until the gelatine has dissolved. Remove from the heat and stir in the honey, vanilla extract and a pinch of salt until dissolved. Taste, and add some rose water if you would like a stronger rose flavour.

Pour the liquid into the bowl of a stand mixer and allow it to cool to room temperature. Using the balloon whisk attachment on your stand mixer, start whisking the marshmallow on a low speed and gradually increase to high as the marshmallow thickens. Whisk for around 10 minutes, until soft, glossy peaks form. Don't over-whisk, or you'll end up with a rubbery (but tasty) mess.

Using a spatula coated in coconut oil, scrape the mix into the brownie pan and level the surface. Place in the freezer for 20 minutes to set.

Place a length of baking paper on top of a cutting board and dust with arrowroot powder. Invert the brownie pan onto the board and peel away the baking paper stuck to the marshmallow.

- 2 tablespoons dried marshmallow root
- 1 tablespoon dried rose petals
- 1 tablespoon dried hibiscus (you can use the contents of an organic teabag)
- 3 tablespoons gelatine powder
- 350 g (12½ oz) honey (local if you can get it) or maple syrup
- ¼ teaspoon vanilla extract
- 1 teaspoon rose water (optional)
- arrowroot powder or grated coconut for dusting

Cut into portions using a sharp knife coated in coconut oil or arrowroot powder.

Toss the marshmallows through arrowroot or grated coconut.

If your marshmallows last long enough – store in an airtight container in the freezer or fridge. Bring to room temperature before serving.

💡 **Coating your utensils in coconut oil or arrowroot will stop them from sticking to the marshmallow.**

Horseradish

Armoracia rusticana

Horseradish promotes the production of gastric secretions, supporting the healthy digestion of fats and protein. A poultice of freshly grated horseradish root wrapped in gauze and placed on skin that has been coated in olive oil can help ease chest congestion. 'Fire cider' is a popular decongestant made from horseradish mixed with other pungent herbs and infused in vinegar. Horseradish is also helpful for sore, swollen joints and gout. Apply until a sensation of warmth is felt. Be cautious as it may cause a rash and blistering.

- **Sow** spring, winter
- **Aspect** full sun to partial shade
- **Spacing** 45–60 cm (18–23 inches)
- **Height** 90 cm (35 inches)
- **Frost & drought** drought tolerant, frost tolerant
- **Soil pH** 6.0–7.0
- **Part used** flower, leaf, root
- **Preparation** food, poultice, tincture
- **Good for** musculoskeletal, respiratory
- **Caution** avoid high doses with peptic ulcers, pregnancy, hypothyroidism

Sow and grow

The easiest way to grow horseradish is from root cuttings. Make a little trench for the rootlet around 3 cm (1¼ inches) deep and place it horizontally, with any shoots facing upwards. Shoots should appear in 2–4 weeks.

Horseradish likes moist, well-drained, rich soil. It prefers cool, moist conditions and may not do too well in hot and dry climates.

Horseradish leaves will die down as the cooler winter weather hits.

Harvest

You can harvest horseradish 6–8 months after planting, but for bigger roots you'll need to wait 2–3 years.

Horseradish roots are ready to harvest in late autumn or early winter. The roots will taste better after a heavy frost has killed off its leafy greens. Harvest the leaves during the growing season from spring to summer. Finely chop the leaves and add them to vegetable dishes for a pungent kick. The pretty yellow flowers are delicious, too, and make a great garnish.

When using horseradish, it is best to let it sit for 3–5 minutes before adding it to your dish. This will give the full benefit of its pungency, heat and medicinal action. If you are preparing horseradish but not going to use it straight away, use vinegar to slow down the oxidisation process, or place it in an airtight container in the fridge. You can freeze grated horseradish in ice cube trays for use at a later date, although it may be a little less intense in heat.

Horseradish is sensitive to heat, and will lose its flavour and pungency when cooked, so most recipes use horseradish raw.

Wood betony

Betonica officinalis

Betony was traditionally used for ailments of the nervous system. It has a mild relaxing affect, easing headaches, nervous tension and anxiety. A compress of strong betony tea or poultice of fresh leaves may be helpful for healing small cuts, grazes and wounds. The bitter and aromatic taste of betony can help to improve digestion and relieve flatulence and bloating, especially when added to other carminative herbs such as lemon balm, sage and peppermint.

- **Sow** spring
- **Aspect** full sun to partial shade
- **Spacing** 30–45 cm (12–18 inches)
- **Height** 60 cm (23 inches)
- **Frost & drought** drought tolerant, frost tolerant
- **Soil pH** 6.0–7.5
- **Part used** flower, leaf
- **Preparation** compress, food, tea, tincture, wash
- **Good for** nervous

Sow and grow

Add betony seeds to fine sand and scatter them on the prepared garden bed. Tamp down lightly so the seeds make contact with the soil and cover lightly with soil. Shoots should appear in 2–4 weeks.

Betony prefers moist, well-draining soils that are rich in organic matter, similar to that of its native woodland habitat. It prefers cooler climates and should be planted in a shadier position in hotter climates. Keep the soil evenly moist during dry spells.

Divide every few years to reduce root congestion and clumping.

Harvest

Betony should be mature enough to harvest in 16–20 weeks.

To harvest your betony plant, cut the leaf and flower stems 2–3 cm (1 inch) above the base of the plant. Harvest the leaves just before the flowers bloom, and flowers as they are newly opened.

Store dried betony in an airtight container for up to 2 years.

Beetroot, berry and betony salad

Serves 2–4

The spicy, pungent earthiness of wood betony complements the roasted beetroot, bitter radicchio and sweet sharpness of the berries in this brightly coloured salad.

To make the vinaigrette, place all of the ingredients in a food processor and blitz until smooth. Set aside for at least the time it takes for the beetroots to roast. Leave longer for a deeper flavour.

To make the salad, preheat the oven to 200°C (390°F) fan-forced and line a baking tray with baking paper.

Place the beetroot on the baking tray with a drizzle of extra-virgin olive oil and a pinch of sea salt and freshly ground black pepper. Roast for 30 minutes, until tender and starting to caramelise on the edges.

Meanwhile, remove the core from the radicchio and cut it into wedges. Heat a little olive oil in a frying pan over medium heat and add the radicchio. Cook for 2–3 minutes, or until it just becomes tender and the red edges start to brown a little.

Lightly toast the sunflower seeds in a small frying pan.

To assemble the salad, lay the radicchio on a large platter (or in individual serving bowls), then scatter over the beetroot and radish. Next, sprinkle the onion, blueberries and herbs. Add the brie and scatter the toasted sunflower seeds. Just before serving, spoon the dressing over the salad and season with sea salt and freshly ground black pepper.

You can make the vinaigrette ahead of time and store it in the fridge for up to 3 days.

Blackberry jam vinaigrette
2 tablespoons extra-virgin olive oil
2 tablespoons balsamic vinegar
1 tablespoon blackberry jam
1 teaspoon wholegrain mustard

Salad
2 beetroots, peeled and cut into 1 inch cubes
extra-virgin olive oil, for drizzling
½ radicchio
¼ cup sunflower seeds, toasted
3–4 radishes, quartered
1 red onion, finely sliced
155 g (5½ oz) blueberries
1 tablespoon young betony leaves, finely sliced
7 g (¼ oz) flat-leaf parsley leaves, finely sliced
5 g (⅛ oz) mint leaves, finely sliced
½ round of brie, cut into thin slices

Calendula

Calendula officinalis

Calendula is well known as a soothing and healing topical remedy. Its antiseptic, anti-inflammatory and tissue regenerative properties nurture and repair damaged skin. It can provide relief for inflamed and irritated skin conditions like rashes and sunburn, as well as helping to speed up wound repair. Calendula can be used as a mouthwash for inflamed gums and mouth ulcers. Pair it with thyme and sage for a soothing throat gargle or spray. Calendula can assist a sluggish lymphatic system, helping the body's immune system fight off infections.

- **Sow** summer, autumn, spring
- **Aspect** full sun to partial shade
- **Spacing** 20–30 cm (8–12 inches)
- **Height** 50 cm (20 inches)
- **Frost & drought** drought tolerant, frost tolerant
- **Soil pH** 6.0–7.0
- **Part used** flower
- **Preparation** compress, food, tea, tincture, wash
- **Good for** lymphatic, skin
- **Caution** known allergen

Sow and grow

Sow the crescent-shaped calendula seeds at a depth of 1.5 cm (⅝ inch). Shoots should appear in around 2 weeks.

Calendula grows well in most soils, as long as they are well drained and contain some rich organic matter.

Calendula readily self-seeds, so you will never be without new plants. Regularly harvest or deadhead spent flowers to encourage more blooms.

Once your plant gets leggy, remove it from the garden bed and pop it in the compost.

Harvest

Calendula flowers should be mature enough to harvest in 8–10 weeks.

Harvest whole blooms throughout the flowering season, including the green, resin-rich calyx. Picking the whole flower helps to maintain its medicinal properties for longer. Calendula will produce new blooms every few days, so keep on top of picking them to encourage new flushes of flowers.

Store dried calendula in an airtight container in a dry, dark place for 1–2 years.

Calendula butter biscuits

Makes 12

These short, buttery biscuits are perfect for dunking into your favourite herbal cuppa. Calendula petals add a touch of sunshine and a mild honeyed flavour. For an extra special treat, you can dip the cookies in melted dark chocolate.

250 g (9 oz) unsalted butter, softened
75 g (2¾ oz) icing (confectioners') sugar, sifted
20 g (¾ oz) dried calendula petals
½ teaspoon vanilla extract
250 g (9 oz) plain (all-purpose) flour, sifted

In a stand mixer fitted with the paddle attachment, cream the butter and icing sugar until pale and creamy.

Use a food processor to blitz the calendula petals into a powder.

Add the powdered calendula and vanilla to the butter and beat to combine well. Add the flour and beat until a soft dough forms.

Refrigerate the dough for 30 minutes.

Preheat the oven to 160°C (320°F) fan-forced. Line a baking tray with baking paper.

Use a spoon to scoop the dough into walnut-sized balls and place them on the baking tray. Lightly press a fork onto the top of each ball.

Bake for 10–15 minutes, until light golden brown.

Let the biscuits rest for a few minutes before transferring them to a wire rack to cool.

Store the biscuits in an airtight container for up to 5 days.

Gotu kola

Centella asiatica

Gotu kola can be used to improve mental clarity, cognitive function and focus. In Ayurvedic medicine, gotu kola is known as a mental rejuvenator. Compounds in gotu kola can stimulate skin repair and growth, as well as increase collagen production. This can provide relief from the symptoms of psoriasis, eczema, burns and wounds. The herb is well known as a helpful remedy for relieving the symptoms of arthritis and reducing joint inflammation. Gotu kola is a part of the carrot family and has a taste similar to carrots, parsley and parsnip.

- **Sow** summer, spring
- **Aspect** full sun to partial shade
- **Spacing** 15–30 cm (6–12 inches)
- **Height** 20 cm (8 inches)
- **Frost & drought** drought tender, frost tender
- **Soil pH** 6.0–7.5
- **Part used** leaf
- **Preparation** compress, food, tea, tincture, wash
- **Good for** cardiovascular, nervous, skin
- **Caution** known allergen

Sow and grow

Soak gotu kola seeds overnight. The next day, rinse and dry the seeds before sowing at a depth of 6 mm (¼ inch). Shoots should appear in 3–6 weeks.

Gotu kola is also easily grown by dividing up established clumps of mature plants.

Although gotu kola loves moist conditions, it needs a really well-draining soil that is rich in organic matter. If the plant has had too much water, the leaves will discolour with yellow and brown spots appearing. Cut these back and let the soil dry out a little between watering. During the growing season, fertilise gotu kola regularly with fish emulsion, seaweed solution or weed tea.

Gotu kola spreads easily, making a lush, green ground cover.

Harvest

Gotu kola should be ready to harvest in 11–13 weeks.

Regular harvesting of the leaves will ensure a continual and abundant supply. Use scissors to harvest the gotu kola, much like giving it a haircut.

Store dried gotu kola leaves in airtight containers for up to 2 years.

Gotu kola salad

Serves 4

This bright zesty salad is a version of a popular Sri Lankan gotu kola sambal. It is traditionally served alongside rice and curry dishes.

Place all the ingredients except the lime juice and extra-virgin olive oil in a serving bowl and mix well. Drizzle on some extra-virgin olive oil and the lime juice. Season with sea salt and freshly ground black pepper, to taste.

Toss the salad just before serving.

If you can't get fresh coconut, you can use shredded coconut – just make sure it doesn't have any added sugar on the ingredients list. Rehydrate it a little in the lime juice before adding it to the salad.

handful of fresh gotu kola leaves, finely chopped
handful of mint leaves, finely chopped
handful of flat-leaf parsley leaves, finely chopped
½ red onion, finely diced
1 green chilli, finely diced, to taste
1 carrot, grated
45 g (1½ oz) fresh coconut, grated
grated zest and juice of 1 lime
extra-virgin olive oil, for drizzling

Hawthorn

Crataegus monogyna

Hawthorn cares for our emotional heart, supporting us through times of grief and loss. Hawthorn berries, flowers and leaves were used traditionally to maintain heart health and circulation. It is a gentle and nourishing remedy for heart-related disorders such palpitations, high blood pressure and irregular heartbeat.

- **Source** foraged, wild-grown
- **Part used** berry, flower, leaf
- **Preparation** food, tea, tincture
- **Good for** cardiovascular
- **Caution** avoid if using beta-blockers, digitalis-based drugs, heart medications

Harvest

The leaves, flowers and berries of hawthorn can be used both fresh and dried.

Leaves and flowers are best gathered when blossoms first start appearing.

Harvest the berries when they are dark red, after the first frost. Remove the berries from the stems.

The dried berries are very hard and may require a mortar and pestle to give them a good crush.

Store the dried flowers, leaves and berries in an airtight container for up to 2 years.

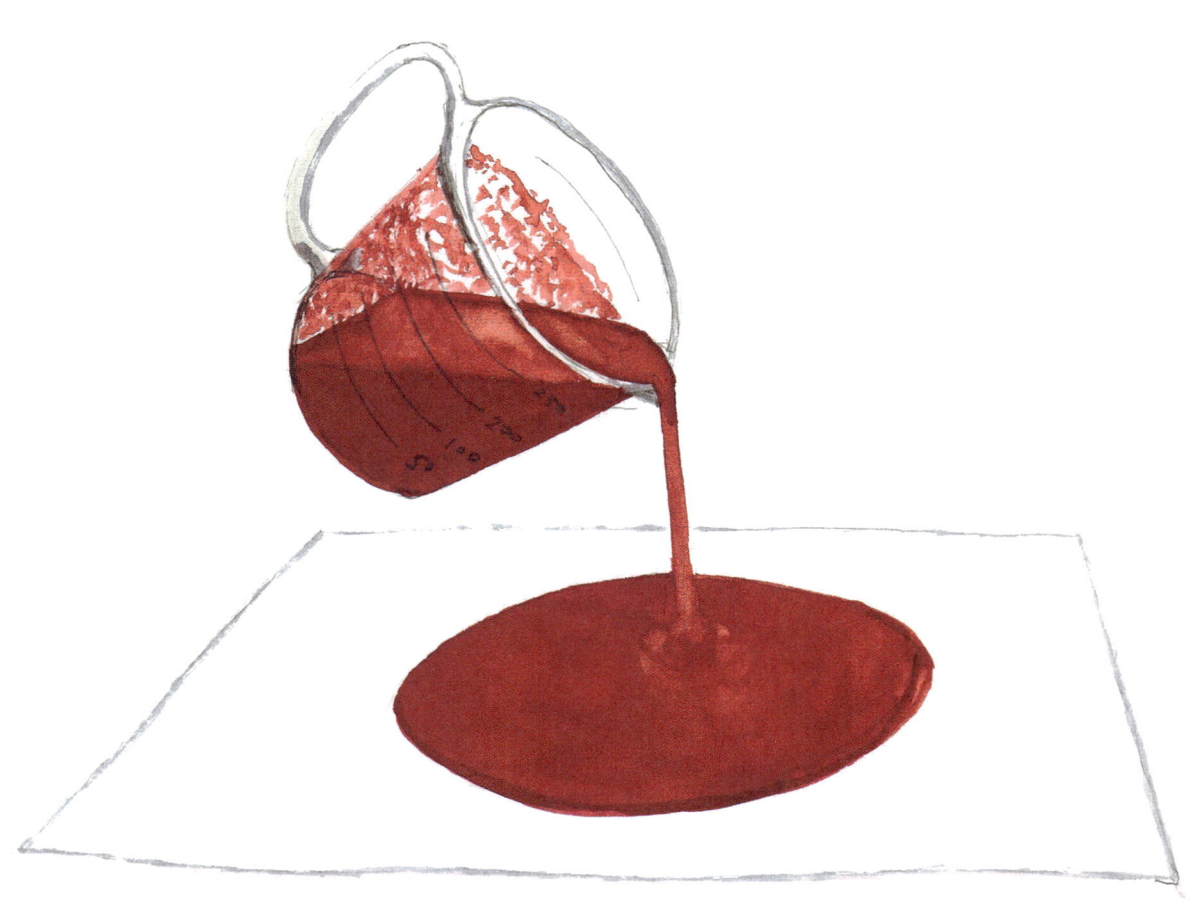

Spiced hawthorn and apple fruit leather

Makes 200–300 g (7–10½ oz)

Three fruits from the same plant family come together in this fruit leather. Have a play with the flavours in this recipe. Remove the rosehips if you don't have any. Change the spices up. If you happen upon some yummy blackberries on your foraging adventures, add these in too.

Fruit leather makes a great walking snack or lunch box treat for the kids.

125 g (4½ oz) dried rosehips
500 g (1 lb 2 oz) fresh hawthorn berries
500 g (1 lb 2 oz) apples, cored and roughly chopped
2 whole dried cloves
½ teaspoon ground cinnamon
¼ teaspoon ground nutmeg
1 tablespoon honey, to taste (local if you can get it)

....

Place the rosehips and 250 ml (8 fl oz) of water in a small saucepan and bring to a gentle simmer. Simmer for 15 minutes, mashing them with a fork while they soften. Once they are soft and pulpy, strain through a muslin-lined sieve to remove the irritating hairs and seeds. Compost the remaining hairs and seeds. The strained liquid will go towards making the fruit leather. Set aside.

In a large stockpot, bring the hawthorn berries, apple, rosehip pulp, spices and 250 ml (8 fl oz) of water to a gentle simmer over medium–low heat. Once simmering, pop the lid on and cook for around 15 minutes, or until the fruit is soft and squishy. Once the fruit is cooked, remove the pot from the heat and mash the fruit with a potato masher until paste-like.

Remove the seeds and skin from the cooked fruit by pushing it through a muslin-lined sieve.

Taste the pulp and add some honey if needed while the mixture is still warm.

Pour the pulp onto lined dehydrator trays and spread it out evenly to around 3–4 mm (⅛ inch) thick using a rubber spatula. Place the trays in the dehydrator on 45°C (113°F) for 8–12 hours for the leather to dry. Alternatively, pop the tray in a dry, warm spot for a few days. Turn the leather as needed to help with drying.

Once the leather has fully dried, cut it into strips. Store the leather in an airtight container in a cool, dark place for up to 1 month. Store in the freezer for up to 12 months.

Turmeric

Curcuma longa

Turmeric is renowned for its anti-inflammatory properties. It can assist with reducing the symptoms of chronic inflammatory conditions such as eczema, psoriasis and asthma, and can be used to support healthy joint function. A homemade turmeric paste can be used to make poultices and balms to use externally. Apply to swollen and sore joints or use it to help speed up the healing of strains and bruises. In traditional Ayurvedic medicine, turmeric is said to ignite the digestive fire, and is used to treat sluggish digestive function and ease travel sickness, nausea and upset stomachs.

- **Sow** summer, spring
- **Aspect** full sun to partial shade
- **Spacing** 30–45 cm (12–18 inches)
- **Height** 100 cm (39 inches)
- **Frost & drought** drought tender, frost tender
- **Soil pH** 6.0–7.5
- **Part used** rhizome
- **Preparation** food, poultice, tea, tincture
- **Good for** digestive, musculoskeletal, skin
- **Caution** taking anti-platelet drugs

Sow and grow

Grow turmeric from seed rhizomes. In cooler climates, plant turmeric rhizomes in pots horizontally, with the growing nodules facing upwards and the soil just covering the rhizomes. Cover with a cloche until shoots appear, in around 4 weeks. In tropical and subtropical regions, plant the rhizomes at a depth of 5–7 cm (2–2¾ inches) directly into prepared beds. Shoots should appear in 6–8 weeks.

Turmeric loves moist, humid conditions but hates having soggy roots. Turmeric grows as a perennial in tropical and subtropical climates, and more like an annual in cooler climates.

Harvest

Turmeric is ready to harvest in 7–10 months from planting.

Yellowing lower leaves or stems that are drying out are signs the plant is old enough to harvest. You can harvest the whole plant, or gently dig down and remove a few pieces as you need. Cut the stems 1–2 cm (½–¾ inches) from the top of the rhizome.

Store fresh turmeric at room temperature or in the fridge. Leave the skin on until you are ready to use it. For longer term storage, grate the turmeric and store it as individual serves in ice cube trays in the freezer.

To dry turmeric, finely slice and place in a single layer on a tray until crispy – it should snap when you break it. Store the pieces whole in an airtight container and grind to a powder as needed.

Frozen turmeric will keep for up to 6 months and dried will keep for up to 2 years.

Spicy cauliflower bites

Serves 4 as a side dish or snack

No matter your dietary preferences, you'll be sure to love these spicy cauliflower bites. They make a great side dish or party snack served with a dipping sauce.

Use stainless steel and non-porous equipment when processing turmeric, as it will stain pretty much anything it comes in contact with.

....

Preheat the oven to 180°C (360°F) fan-forced and line a baking tray with baking paper.

In a medium bowl add the flour, almond meal, spices, nutritional yeast and a pinch each of sea salt and freshly ground black pepper. Pour in 185 ml (6 fl oz) of water and the olive oil and stir until it forms a batter. Add more water if it is needed.

Using a fork to hold the cauliflower pieces, dip them in the batter to coat them, then place them on the baking tray.

Bake for 20 minutes, or until golden and crispy.

Place the crispy cauliflower bites into a serving dish and sprinkle with a good pinch of sea salt. Serve as is, or accompanied by aioli, sweet chilli sauce or your favourite dipping sauce.

65 g (2¼ oz) manioc flour (cassava flour)
25 g (1 oz) almond meal
2 teaspoons turmeric powder
1 teaspoon smoked paprika powder
1 teaspoon garlic powder
pinch cayenne powder
1 teaspoon nutritional yeast
2 teaspoons extra-virgin olive oil
½ cauliflower head, chopped into bite-size pieces
aioli or sweet chilli sauce, to serve (optional)

Globe artichoke

Cynara scolymus

In herbal medicine, globe is known as a bitter liver tonic, meaning it helps support healthy liver and digestive function; relieving bloating, cramps and flatulence. It can be used to relieve the symptoms of irritable bowel syndrome. Globe keeps good gut bacteria happy by feeding them with prebiotic fibre. Eating and using herbal preparations of globe artichoke stimulates the gall bladder, helping the body break down fatty food and maintain healthy cholesterol.

- **Sow** spring
- **Aspect** full sun
- **Spacing** 90–120 cm (35–47 inches)
- **Height** 160 cm (63 inches)
- **Frost & drought** frost tender, mildly drought tolerant
- **Soil pH** 6.5–7.5
- **Part used** leaf
- **Preparation** food, tea, tincture
- **Good for** digestive
- **Caution** known allergen

Sow and grow

Sow globe seeds at a depth of 1 cm (½ inch). Shoots should appear in around 3 weeks.

Globe artichoke can take at least a year to mature. For faster maturing plants, grow globe by root division of mature plants or plant out their suckers in spring.

Globe like moist, well-drained, rich soil. In colder climates, they will die down in winter. Mulch around the crown to protect them from heavy frost.

After your first harvest, cut the plant right back to the ground and you'll get a second crop. Give it a good feed with fertiliser and some mulch.

Harvest

Harvest globe artichoke when it is young and before the plant flowers. Harvest the flower buds for eating fresh while young and succulent. Make sure they're a good eating size, but pick before the flower buds open.

Leave a few flowers on the plants as they will readily self-seed and the bees and butterflies will love the purple blooms. The dried flower stems also make lovely dried arrangements.

Store dried leaves in an airtight container for up to 2 years.

Echinacea

Echinacea spp.

Most of us know of echinacea as a remedy for immune system support, especially in the treatment of colds. Herbalists use the immune-enhancing and antiseptic properties of echinacea for the treatment of urinary tract infections. Echinacea can be used externally on infected cuts and wounds, psoriasis and eczema. A strong tea or diluted tincture can be gargled as a mouthwash to assist in healing ulcers and gingivitis.

- **Sow** autumn, spring
- **Aspect** full sun
- **Spacing** 30–45 cm (12–18 inches)
- **Height** 80 cm (31 inches)
- **Frost & drought** drought tolerant, frost tolerant
- **Soil pH** 6.0–7.0
- **Part used** flower, leaf, root
- **Preparation** compress, food, tincture, wash
- **Good for** immune, lymphatic, respiratory, skin
- **Caution** known allergen

Varieties
Echinacea angustifolia – purple cone flower
Echinacea pallida – narrow leaf cone flower
Echinacea purpurea – pale purple cone flower

Sow and grow
Stratify echinacea seeds for a month before sowing at a depth of 6 mm (¼ inch). Echinacea can be slow to germinate, but shoots should appear in 2–3 weeks.

Echinacea will self-seed if you let it. You can propagate by dividing the roots in late autumn or winter. Choose mature plants that are 2–3 years old.

Echinacea likes moist, well-drained, rich soil. For a beautiful flush of flowers, give them a regular feed and water and encourage abundant blooms by regularly deadheading.

Cut back dead flower heads and leaves in late autumn, as the plant will die down over winter. Mulch to protect the crown from frost and make sure it doesn't get too soggy during winter. You may not get a flush of flowers in the first season while the plant is busy growing and storing energy in its roots.

Harvest
Echinacea should be ready to harvest 13–20 weeks from planting. Harvest the flowers in summer and the leaves as needed.

When harvesting, only take a quarter of the leaves and flowers at a time. This enables the plant to store important energy in its roots for its dormancy over winter. Harvest the root in late autumn in the third or fourth year of growth.

Store dried echinacea in an airtight container in a dry, dark place for 1–2 years.

Echinacea, ginger and thyme syrup

Makes 500 ml (17 fl oz)

Make this syrup and keep it in the fridge to take at the first sign of a cold or flu. For a cold, take 1–2 teaspoons of the syrup three times per day or just enjoy a spoonful in a mug of hot water any time.

Place the echinacea, thyme, ginger, lemon zest and juice in a small saucepan. Add the water and bring to a boil over medium heat, then reduce the heat to low. Place a lid loosely on the pot and simmer for 15–20 minutes, or until the liquid has reduced by half.

Remove from the heat and strain through a fine mesh sieve into a heatproof jug. Push the herbs with the back of a spoon to squeeze out excess liquid. Discard the spent herbs into your compost.

Add the honey and stir until dissolved. Let the syrup cool, then stir in the brandy (if using). Pour the syrup through a funnel into sterilised bottles and secure the lids.

The syrup will keep in the fridge for 2–3 months.

1 cup whole dried echinacea plant, roughly chopped, or 2 cups fresh
1 bunch thyme sprigs
50 g (1¾ oz) ginger, peeled and grated
zest of ½ lemon
juice of 1 lemon
1 litre (34 fl oz) filtered water
500 ml (17 fl oz) raw honey (local if you can get it)
3 tablespoons brandy (optional)

✱ **Caution** Honey should not be given to children under the age of one.

California poppy

Eschscholzia californica

California poppy is a beautiful herb to reach for when you are feeling too wound up for sleep. It is often used with other calming and relaxing herbs, such as chamomile, hops, lavender and skullcap to help ease anxiety and nervous tension. California poppy is non-addictive and was traditionally used to ease nerve and muscle pain. It can be used to assist with the relief of menstrual pain, toothaches and tension headaches.

- **Sow** summer, spring
- **Aspect** full sun
- **Spacing** 15–30 cm (6–12 inches)
- **Height** 40 cm (16 inches)
- **Frost & drought** drought tolerant, frost tolerant
- **Soil pH** 6.0–8.0
- **Part used** flower, leaf, root, seed
- **Preparation** food, tea, tincture
- **Good for** nervous
- **Caution** avoid during pregnancy and if taking MAOIs (monoamine oxidase inhibitor)

Sow and grow

Scatter California poppy seeds directly onto prepared garden beds, as they don't like having their roots disturbed. Shoots should appear in 2–3 weeks.

It prefers sandy, well-drained soil, and won't do well if its roots get too wet. If you have clay soil, it's probably best to plant your poppies in raised beds or pots – but note they will need more regular watering than if planted directly into the ground.

It readily self-seeds. The plant will die down over winter, with new seedlings popping up in spring.

California poppy grows well with chamomile and calendula.

Harvest

California poppy is ready to harvest in 10–12 weeks.

The freshly harvested flowers are fairly delicate and fall apart easily. The bright orange colour fades quickly once dried, so you will need to keep them out of the light. Use dark amber glass bottles and jars stored in a dark cupboard. Use the flowers sooner than later.

Harvest the leaves as you need during the growing season and the roots in late autumn. Harvest the long seed pods just before they're fully dry and about to open. They will have just turned from green to brown. The ridges along the seed pod will also become more visible when they're ready to harvest. Place the pods in a paper bag with the top rolled down.

Store dried California poppy in an airtight container in a dry, dark place for 1–2 years.

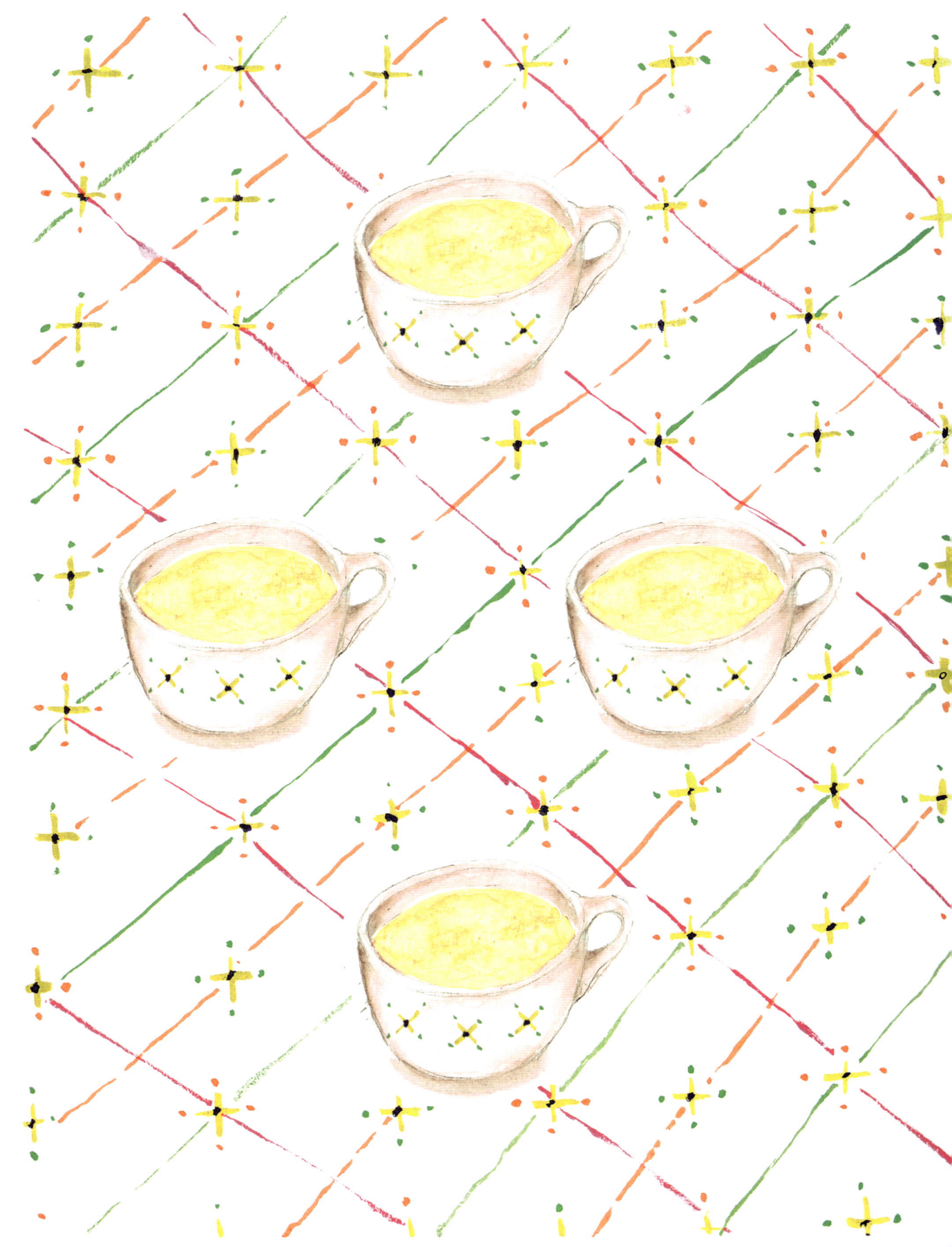

California poppy sweet dreams milk

Serves 2

Did you ever have warm milk and honey as a little kid to help you settle in ready for bed? Here's an updated version with some beautiful, calming and relaxing herbs to send you off for the sweetest of dreams.

Use a food processor or mortar and pestle to grind the California poppy, tulsi and rose petals into a powder.

Pour the milk into a small saucepan along with the herb powder, cinnamon, coconut oil and a pinch of salt. Cover with a lid and bring to a gentle simmer on medium heat. Simmer for 5 minutes, or until your desired drinking temperature is reached.

Strain the milk and discard the leaves, then add honey, to taste. Use a stick blender to blitz the milk until nice and frothy.

To serve, pour the warm milk into mugs and dust with cinnamon and a sprinkle of rose petals.

2 teaspoons dried California poppy leaves and/or stems

2 teaspoons dried tulsi leaves

2 teaspoons dried rose petals, plus extra for sprinkling

500 ml (17 fl oz) milk (dairy or non-dairy)

½ teaspoon ground cinnamon, plus extra for dusting

1 teaspoon coconut oil

honey or maple syrup, to taste

Meadowsweet

Filipendula ulmaria

Aspirin was originally derived from meadowsweet. The salicylic acid in meadowsweet gives it pain-relieving and anti-inflammatory benefits, making it useful in the treatment of muscular and arthritic pain, pounding headaches, feverish colds and cystitis. It has a much gentler and friendlier effect on the digestive system than aspirin does. Meadowsweet is a great herb for digestive complaints. It soothes the mucous membranes throughout the digestive tract, providing relief from indigestion, heartburn and nausea. It can settle stomach-aches, reduce flatulence and bloating, ease diarrhoea and assist in healing stomach ulcers.

- **Sow** autumn, spring
- **Aspect** full sun to partial shade
- **Spacing** 45–60 cm (18–23 inches)
- **Height** 60–90 cm (23–35 inches)
- **Frost & drought** drought tolerant, frost tolerant
- **Soil pH** 5.5–7.0
- **Part used** flower
- **Preparation** food, tea, tincture
- **Good for** digestive, nervous, respiratory
- **Caution** aspirin sensitivity, taking warfarin

Sow and grow

Meadowsweet is best propagated by root division in spring and autumn. It loves rich, moist, but well-drained soils.

Meadowsweet bushes flower in summer through to autumn. Deadhead to encourage further blooming. After the flowering season, trim the stems down to 5–10 cm (2–4 inches) above the ground.

In colder climates, meadowsweet may completely die back to the ground in winter, but new shoots will appear in spring.

Harvest

Meadowsweet flowers should be ready to harvest in around 90–120 days. Choose flowers that have fully opened and are the most fragrant. Leaves can be harvested as you need them.

The fragrance of the flowers intensifies when they are dried.

Store dried meadowsweet in an airtight container for up to 2 years.

Meadowsweet and rhubarb crumble with meadowsweet custard

Serves 4

In this twist on a classic dessert, meadowsweet and rhubarb compote is topped with a biscuity crumble. The custard imparts a sweet fragrance reminiscent of almond essence.

For the compote, place the rhubarb, sugar, vanilla, meadowsweet flowers and lemon juice and peel into a medium saucepan with 80 ml (2½ fl oz) of water over low heat, stirring until the sugar dissolves. Turn the heat up to bring to a boil and cook for 4 minutes. Remove the saucepan from the heat and set aside until cool.

For the crumble, preheat the oven to 180°C (360°F) fan-forced and grease a 2-litre (68 fl oz) baking dish.

Combine the flour, almond meal, sugar and cinnamon in a large bowl. Rub in the butter using your fingertips until well combined. It will be like a thick biscuit dough. Mix in the nuts and seeds.

Remove the meadowsweet flowers, lemon peel and vanilla pod from the compote and discard. Spoon the compote into the baking dish. Squish bits of the crumble mixture over the top of the compote evenly. Sprinkle with a little brown sugar, and bake for 25 minutes, or until the crumble is golden.

While the crumble is in the oven, make the custard. Gently heat the milk, cream, meadowsweet flowers and lemon rind together in a large saucepan over medium–low heat. Turn the heat off just as it comes to a gentle simmer and stir in the honey. Set aside for 15 minutes to cool a little. Strain the infused milk over a medium bowl. In a large bowl, whisk together the eggs and the sugar. Pour in the infused milk, making sure to keep whisking the whole time.

Strain this mixture into a large, clean saucepan and warm over low heat; you don't want the custard to boil. Keep stirring until the custard has reached your desired consistency.

Remove the crumble from the oven when it is ready and allow it to cool for around 10 minutes (the compote gets volcanic!) before serving with meadowsweet custard. This will keep in the fridge for around 2 days.

6 rhubarb stalks, chopped into bite-size pieces
110 g (4 oz) white (granulated) sugar
½ vanilla pod
handful of meadowsweet flowers
juice of 1 lemon, plus a strip of peel (orange works well too)
50 g (1¾ oz) plain (all-purpose) flour (use gluten-free if needed)
35 g (1¼ oz) almond meal
60 g (2 oz) soft brown sugar, plus 1 teaspoon more for sprinkling
1 teaspoon ground cinnamon
90 g (3 oz) salted butter
¼ cup mixed chopped nuts and seeds

Meadowsweet custard
250 ml (8½ fl oz) full-cream (whole) milk
250 ml (8½ fl oz) pure cream
handful of fresh meadowsweet flowers
1 strip of lemon rind
1 tablespoon honey
3 eggs
2 tablespoons caster sugar

 The compote also tastes great served on top of your morning porridge with a dollop of natural yoghurt, or used in cakes and muffins. The meadowsweet custard can be churned into delicious ice cream.

Fennel

Foeniculum vulgare

Sweet fennel can be used for supporting digestion; calming upset, cramping and flatulent tummies. Infuse the seeds in honey and stir into hot water or herbal tea for a lovely anise-flavoured brew. Chew a couple of seeds for a sweet anise hit that freshens breath and settles indigestion. Fennel can help to soothe the spasm of coughs and bronchitis, and assist with easing chest congestion. Make a herbal spray to help heal mouth ulcers, inflamed gums and sore throats. You can use fennel in savoury and sweet dishes. Add fennel at the end of cooking to highlight its flavour, and remember, a little bit goes a long way.

- **Sow** summer, autumn, spring
- **Aspect** full sun to partial shade
- **Spacing** 30–45 cm (12–18 inches)
- **Height** 120 cm (47 inches)
- **Frost & drought** frost and drought tolerant
- **Soil pH** 6.0–7.0
- **Part used** flower, leaf
- **Preparation** food, tea, tincture
- **Good for** digestive, lactation, respiratory
- **Caution** gastro-oesophageal reflux

Varieties
Foeniculum vulgare var. *dulce* – Florence fennel

Sow and grow
Sow seeds directly in beds at a depth of 8 mm (5/16 inch). Shoots should appear in around 2 weeks.

Fennel grows in most soil conditions, but prefers moist, rich, well-drained soil.

Fennel is a cool-season crop, grown as an annual by most gardeners. It may bolt in hot weather. Fennel readily self-seeds and can become weedy. Deadhead flowers to collect the pollen and seeds – and to stop prolific self-seeding. Removing the flowers also keeps the rest of the plant sweeter in flavour.

Harvest
Fennel will be ready to harvest in 11–13 weeks.

Even though the bulbs of sweet fennel are smaller than Florence fennel, they can still be utilised the same way when used as a food ingredient. Harvest bulbs in autumn and the fresh fronds as you need.

Harvest the pollen before the fennel flowers go to seed. Look for bright yellow flower heads where most of the florets have opened. Cut the flowers off and pop them in a paper bag. Shake the bag to release the pollen to the bottom. The dried flowers make a beautiful, tasty garnish.

Always store dried fennel in airtight containers, as exposure to air rapidly decreases its sweet anise aromatic oil. Dried seeds and pollen will keep for up to 2 years; dried flowers and leaves for up to 12 months.

Nourish fennel cookies

Makes 12

These cookies make for a delicious afternoon tea treat. If you prefer a texture more like an Anzac biscuit, you can keep the oats whole.

Blitz the fennel, aniseed and caraway into a powder using a food processor.

In a stand mixer fitted with the paddle attachment, beat the butter and sugar until pale and creamy. Beat in the eggs, one at a time. Add the maple syrup, vanilla, cinnamon and fennel mix and beat to combine well.

Add the almond meal, oats, flaxseeds, baking powder and a pinch of salt and stir until well combined. Stir in the chocolate chips.

Chill the dough in the fridge for 30 minutes.

Preheat the oven to 170°C (340°F) fan-forced. Line a baking tray with baking paper.

Using a teaspoon, scoop out the cookie dough and shape it into balls. Place them on the baking tray and lightly press the top of each ball to flatten it a little. Bake on the middle shelf of the oven for 10 minutes, until lightly golden.

Remove from the oven and leave the cookies to cool on the tray for a few minutes before transferring to a wire baking rack.

Store in an airtight container for up to 1 week.

- 1 teaspoon fennel seed
- 1 teaspoon aniseed seeds
- ½ teaspoon caraway seeds
- 125 g (4½ oz) unsalted butter, softened
- 140 g (5 oz) soft brown sugar
- 2 eggs
- 1 tablespoon maple syrup
- ½ teaspoon vanilla extract
- 1 teaspoon ground cinnamon
- 200 g (7 oz) almond meal
- 145 g (5 oz) oats, ground
- 1 tablespoon flaxseeds, ground
- 1 teaspoon baking powder
- 125 g (4½ oz) white chocolate chips

Cleavers

Galium aparine

Cleavers pops up and creeps through the garden in spring and autumn. The whole plant is covered in velcro-like hooks that help it cleave and cling to other plants, woolly socks, clothing, fluffy dogs and fences.

- **Source** foraged, wild-grown
- **Part used** leaf, seed
- **Preparation** compress, food, tea, tincture, wash
- **Good for** lymphatic, skin, urinary
- **Caution** known allergen

Cleavers is high in vitamin C and is used in herbal medicine for its anti-inflammatory and antibacterial properties. It's useful in the treatment of skin conditions such as dermatitis, eczema and psoriasis, and is a helpful tonic to counter the effects of rich food.

You can make a succus (juice preserved with alcohol) from the fresh plant and freeze it in ice cube trays to be used as a wash on sunburn, rashes and grazes. Crush the leaves and rub them on the skin for the relief of bug bites and stings.

The seeds can be used as a coffee substitute. An overnight cold brew of cleavers is a great way to start the day and get your lymphatic system in full swing.

Cooking cleavers reduces the sticky texture; and blending it makes it even better in juices, soups and smoothies.

Harvest
Harvest young cleavers shoots and leaves before it goes to seed. Cleavers leaves are best used fresh, but they can be dried also. The seeds can be harvested when they have turned from green to brown, usually in late summer and autumn.

Cleavers coffee

Makes 250 ml (8½ fl oz)

Did you know that cleavers is a member of the coffee family? I would never say anything is an exact substitute for coffee, but this is a really pleasant warm beverage.

60 g (2 oz) dried cleavers seeds

Toast the cleavers seeds in a heavy based frying pan over a low heat. Stir the seeds frequently, being careful not to let them catch and burn. They will be ready when they have a sweet, malty, coffee-like smell.

Let the seeds cool, then store them in an airtight container for up to 12 months. For freshness, grind the seeds using a coffee grinder or mortar and pestle as you need them.

To make a cup of cleavers, place 1 generous teaspoon per cup into a teapot or coffee plunger and top up with boiling water. Let brew for around 5–10 minutes.

Licorice

Glycyrrhiza glabra

Licorice is a herb that helps to improve the body's resistance and response to physical, emotional and environmental stressors – in herbal medicine we call this an adaptogen. Licorice soothes and coats the mucosal linings of the digestive and respiratory tracts. It can calm hot, inflamed and irritated tissue associated with sore throats, coughs, bronchitis and asthma. Licorice can ease digestive discomfort and provide relief from irritable bowel syndrome, constipation, digestive ulcers and heartburn. A wash or compress of strong licorice tea or diluted tincture can be used to alleviate the irritation of eczema, psoriasis and dermatitis.

- **Sow** summer, spring
- **Aspect** full sun to partial shade
- **Spacing** 30–45 cm (12–18 inches)
- **Height** 150 cm (59 inches)
- **Frost & drought** drought tolerant, frost tolerant
- **Soil pH** 6.0–7.5
- **Part used** root
- **Preparation** compress, food, tea, tincture, wash
- **Good for** digestive, respiratory, skin
- **Caution** avoid long-time use of high doses, during pregnancy, lactation, hypertension, hypokalaemia, oedema, congestive heart failure, heart, liver or kidney disease and alongside laxative use

Sow and grow

Licorice is easily propagated by stem cuttings and root division. Licorice is stoloniferous, meaning it will send out horizontal stems that shoot down new roots, creating a new plant in the same way that strawberries do. If you grow plants by root division, the growth will be faster and you'll be able to harvest sooner.

Licorice likes moist, slightly sandy, well-drained soil. It benefits from regular watering, but has the potential to develop root rot if you overwater. If you live in an area of high rainfall, consider growing the plants on mounds or raised beds to help with water drainage.

The plants will die down in cold weather and reshoot in spring. The more warmth the plant is exposed to, the sweeter the taste of the roots.

Harvest

Licorice plants are mature and ready to harvest after 2–3 years of growing.

Harvest roots in autumn, when the plant has died down.

The dried roots will be ready when they are crispy.

Store dried licorice in an airtight container for up to 2 years.

Licorice logs

Makes 12

Did you know your favourite licorice candy was once made from the licorice plant? These days, licorice is made with aniseed flavouring and black food colouring – no licorice at all!

This licorice recipe uses powdered licorice root plus anise-flavoured herbs for an extra-strong flavour. Licorice logs may soothe sore throats and inflamed, upset tummies.

....

Prepare a small baking dish by lining it with baking paper and lightly greasing it with melted coconut oil or vegetable oil.

Use a food processor to blitz the licorice root, anise seeds and star anise pods into a powder. Pass the powdered herbs through a fine mesh sieve to remove any large pieces. Regrind the larger pieces and push those through the sieve again. You want the powder to be as fine as possible.

Place the brown sugar, molasses, butter, powdered herbs and a pinch of salt in a medium saucepan over low heat. Stir with a silicon spatula until the sugar has dissolved. Don't allow the sugar mixture to boil. Add 1 tablespoon of water and stir for 2–3 minutes until well combined.

Add the sifted flour, one tablespoon at a time, stirring constantly until the mix comes together into a thick paste.

Remove from the heat and spoon the paste onto the baking pan. Spread the paste out in an even layer about 5 mm (¼ inch) thick.

Cool the paste in the fridge until you can handle it with bare hands, it should still be warm and malleable.

Transfer to a cutting board and remove the baking paper. Using an oiled knife, cut the licorice into squares or strips to roll and twist together. Toss the licorice through the arrowroot and icing sugar – this will prevent them from sticking together.

Place the licorice in an airtight container and store it in the fridge for up to 1 week.

- 1 tablespoon ground dried licorice root
- 1 teaspoon anise seeds
- 2 star anise pods
- 95 g (3¼ oz) soft brown sugar
- 3 tablespoons blackstrap molasses
- 2 tablespoons unsalted butter
- 35–75 g (1¼–2¾ oz) plain (all-purpose) flour, sifted
- 2 teaspoons each of icing (confectioners') sugar and arrowroot, sifted, for dusting

Hops

Humulus lupulus

In herbal medicine, hops are used primarily for their relaxing action on the nervous system. If you're having trouble sleeping, feeling tense or stressed out, then hops might be a remedy for you. Add hops to a lavender eye pillow (page 82) for extra sedative properties. Place the pillow on your head to help soothe tension headaches, toothaches and earaches. It's also said to prevent nightmares. The bitter taste of hops supports healthy digestive function. Add hops to lemon balm, chamomile or mint herbal tea to ease indigestion.

- **Sow** spring, winter
- **Aspect** full sun to partial shade
- **Spacing** 90–150 cm (35–59 inches)
- **Height** up to 300 cm (9 ft 10 inches)
- **Frost & drought** drought tolerant, frost tolerant
- **Soil pH** 6.0–7.5
- **Part used** flower
- **Preparation** food, tea, tincture
- **Good for** nervous
- **Caution** depression, estrogen-sensitive

Sow and grow

Hops is best grown from rhizomes as you are guaranteed to know the sex of the plant – only the female plant grows the flower cones. Dig a hole in a prepared bed around 10 cm (4 inches) deep. Plant the rhizome in the hole horizontally, or with any visible buds pointing upwards.

It will grow in most soil types, as long as they are well draining and rich in organic matter.

Hops are voracious growers – they can grow up to 30 cm (12 inches) in one day, so train them onto a trellis, winding them in a clockwise direction. Hops will die down in late autumn after flowering. Prune them back to 3 cm (1¼ inches) above the ground.

Divide the plants up every 3 years or so.

Harvest

Hops plants have irritating little hairs, so it's best to wear long sleeves and cover up when you're harvesting them.

The plant won't begin to flower until its second year of growth. Harvest hops flowers in mid- to late summer when they are a light yellow–green colour and the bracts are starting to separate. If you squeeze them, they should feel papery and spring back to shape.

Harvest the shoots in early spring. You'll be able to harvest the shoots for around 2 weeks. Leave the strongest three or four shoots to grow.

Pack dried hops flowers tightly into ziplock bags and squeeze out most of the air. They will keep in the freezer for up to 3 years. If stored at room temperature, use within 6 months.

Hops shoot pickles

Makes 500 ml (17 fl oz)

For fans of pickles and condiments, you're going to love these pickled hops shoots. This recipe uses a simple pickle brine, but you can experiment by adding in your favourite flavours. Hops shoots have the crunchy texture of bean shoots and taste similar to asparagus.

Place the hops shoots into a clean, sterilised jar. In a medium saucepan over high heat, bring the rest of the ingredients and 250 ml (8 fl oz) of water to the boil. Remove from the heat and, using a funnel, carefully pour the hot vinegar over the hops shoots.

Let the vinegar cool completely before putting on the lid and popping it into the fridge. Leave the pickled shoots for at least a week before eating.

The pickles will last in the fridge for up to 6 months.

2 cups of hops shoots
250 ml (8 fl oz) apple cider vinegar or white wine vinegar
2 tablespoons white (granulated) sugar
2 tablespoons salt
5 whole black peppercorns
1 bay leaf
1 teaspoon dill seeds
4 garlic cloves
1 teaspoon chilli flakes (optional)

Lavender

Lavandula

Lavender has long been used to calm nerves and ease headaches. A bedtime bath scattered with lavender buds or a little lavender under the pillow is thought to aid a good night's sleep. Lavender's calming effect extends to digestion; easing gas, bloating and cramping. Cooling washes and compresses of strong lavender tea can soothe sunburn and rashes. The antimicrobial and antiseptic properties of lavender make it a handy first-aid remedy in the treatment of cuts, grazes and itchy bites. Lavender can be used in cooking, but use a light touch when adding it to your culinary creations.

- **Sow** summer, autumn, spring
- **Aspect** full sun
- **Spacing** 30–45 cm (12–18 inches)
- **Height** 120 cm (47 inches)
- **Frost & drought** frost and drought tolerant
- **Soil pH** 6.5–7.5
- **Part used** flower
- **Preparation** compress, food, poultice, tea, tincture, steam inhalation, wash
- **Good for** digestive, nervous, skin
- **Caution** known allergen

Varieties

Lavandula x *intermedia* 'Grosso' – extremely fragrant flowers with a very high essential oil content
Lavandula angustifolia 'Hidcote' – compact dwarf variety with deep, dark purple flowers
Lavandula angustifolia 'Munstead' – shaggy dwarf variety with lighter purple flowers
Lavandula angustifolia 'Vera' – true English lavender

Sow and grow

Lavender is easiest to grow from cuttings. Take cuttings from non-flowering stems in spring and autumn. Roots can take 3–6 weeks to develop. It can also be propagated by layering.

Lavender likes well-drained, moderately fertile, almost sandy soil. It won't tolerate getting soggy feet and is prone to root rot. For greater fragrance, don't overwater or over-fertilise the plants.

Encourage abundant blooms by regularly deadheading. Prune back about two-thirds of the plant's height after the final flush of flowers. Be careful not to cut into the woody stems as you may kill the plant.

Harvest

Lavender is considered mature after 1 year of growing. You may get a small flush of flowers in the first year.

Harvest lavender buds first thing in the early morning, as the aromatic oils decrease with the bloom's age.

To dry, hang the long flower stems in bunches, covered with a paper bag to protect them from light. Store the leaves and flowers in an airtight container for up to 2 years.

Quick lavender eye pillow

Makes 1

This simple lavender eye pillow can help relaxation and relieve headaches. Flaxseeds are added to the filling as they have good heat retention (if you want to warm them up). They also have a lovely, lightweight, flowing feeling through the fabric and mould nicely to the shape of your face.

Try adding different herbs for different effects. Lavender, chamomile and mugwort are good for sleep. Or try lavender, peppermint and feverfew for headaches.

dried lavender flowers

flaxseeds (buckwheat or rice will also work)

25 cm (10 inch) square of flannel, cotton or linen

Place the lavender and flaxseeds in a small bowl and mix to combine.

Lay the piece of fabric on a flat surface, then pile the flowers and seeds into the centre in a heap. Pull up two opposite corners of the square and tie them together in a single knot over the lavender. Do the same thing with the remaining two corners. Now tie the first two corners in another knot. Repeat with the remaining two corners.

Give the pillow a good shake to mix the herbs up. The pillow can be heated in the microwave or used as is.

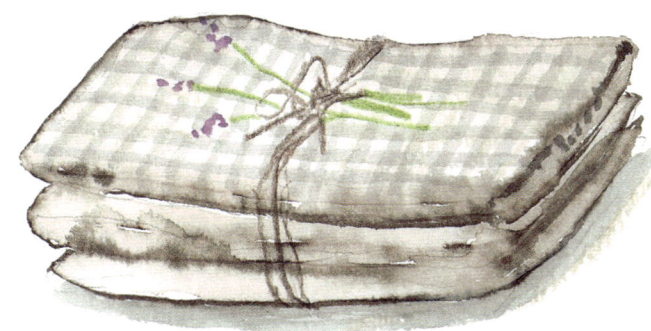

Lavender lemonade scones

Makes 12

Lemonade scones are light and fluffy and traditionally have only three ingredients: flour, lemonade and cream. This recipe features lavender, lemon and vanilla for a truly fragrant scone – but they are still super simple to make.

450 g (1 lb) self-raising flour

2 teaspoons of dried lavender flowers, lightly crushed with a mortar and pestle

½ vanilla pod, seeds scraped out

2 teaspoons of lemon zest

250 ml (8½ fl oz) pure cream

250 ml (8½ fl oz) lemonade

Preheat the oven to 180°C (360°F) fan-forced and line a baking tray with baking paper.

Sift the flour with a pinch of salt into a large mixing bowl, then add in the lavender, vanilla seeds and lemon zest. Use a whisk to combine well.

Pour in the cream and lemonade and quickly mix the dough with a spatula or the blade of a knife.

Turn the dough out onto a floured surface and gently knead together. Form into a ball and roll out to 3 cm (1¼ inch) thick. Use floured cookie cutters or an upside down drinking glass to cut out rounds. Squish the scraps of dough together and repeat until it's all used up.

Place the rounds on the baking tray, brush the tops with a little bit of cream, and bake for 15–20 minutes, until they are lightly golden on top.

Serve with butter, your favourite jam and lashings of thick cream, washed down with your favourite cuppa.

Scones are best eaten on the day you make them. Store in an airtight container in the fridge for up to 2 days. Warm before serving.

Motherwort

Leonurus cardiaca

Traditionally, motherwort was used as a herbal remedy for women in all stages of their lives. The Latin name of motherwort, *Leonurus cardiaca*, means 'lion hearted'. The tincture can be used to assist in the relief of premenstrual syndrome, cramping and pain and may be helpful for some of the symptoms associated with perimenopause such as hot flushes. It may also be helpful for nervous tension and anxiety.

- **Sow** autumn, spring
- **Aspect** full sun to partial shade
- **Spacing** 30–45 cm (12–18 inches)
- **Height** 180 cm (71 inches)
- **Frost & drought** drought tender, frost tolerant
- **Soil pH** 6.0–7.5
- **Part used** flower, leaf
- **Preparation** food, tea, tincture
- **Good for** cardiovascular, nervous, reproductive
- **Caution** pregnancy, heavy menstrual bleeding

Sow and grow

Motherwort seeds benefit from some cold stratification before sowing. Soak the seeds for 24 hours, then place them in the fridge for 10 days. Sow the seeds at a depth of 3 mm (⅛ inch). Shoots should appear in 2–3 weeks.

It readily self-seeds and is easy to propagate by cuttings and root division in spring and autumn.

Plant your motherwort in rich, moist, well-drained soil. It will grow almost anywhere and has become weedy in many areas.

Prune the spent flower heads before they have time to go to seed. Some people prefer to plant motherwort in containers to stop it from spreading through the garden via its vigorous runners.

Harvest

Motherwort should be mature enough to harvest in 12 weeks. Harvest motherwort just as it is beginning to flower. Cut the top third of the flowering stems. Motherwort can be a bit spiky to collect, so wear long sleeves and gloves when harvesting.

Store dried motherwort in an airtight container for up to 2 years.

Bittersweet chocolate truffles

Makes 12

These truffles will take your chocolate hit to another level. We all know a good dose of chocolate can help us cope with just about anything, and the motherwort and rose powders in these truffles add to the soothing effect.

Use at least 70 per cent cacao chocolate for these truffles – there's just enough sweet chocolate flavour to marry with the bitterness of the motherwort.

You can turn these truffle balls into a yummy hot chocolate by plonking one into some warmed milk.

- 150 g (5½ oz) dark chocolate, at least 70 per cent cacao, chopped
- 125 ml (4 fl oz) coconut cream
- 2 teaspoons coconut oil
- 1 teaspoon motherwort powder
- ½ teaspoon ground cinnamon
- 1 teaspoon rose powder
- ½ teaspoon rosewater or 4 drops of rose extract (start off with smaller amounts and add more to taste)
- ¼ teaspoon vanilla extract
- cacao powder, sifted, for rolling
- rose powder for rolling

Place the chocolate into a heatproof bowl. Sit the bowl over a pan of water that has just boiled and been removed from the heat. Stir in the coconut cream and coconut oil and leave to sit for 4 minutes. Stir once again, making sure all of the chocolate has melted and combined with the coconut cream.

Add the motherwort, cinnamon, rose powder, rosewater, vanilla extract and a pinch of salt. Gently stir until well combined.

Pop it in the fridge to cool for 30–60 minutes. (It shouldn't be set hard.)

Line a baking tray with baking paper. Before you start rolling the truffles, coat your hands in a little vegetable oil to stop the chocolate from sticking. Scoop out 2 teaspoons of the truffle mix, quickly roll into balls and place on the baking tray. Continue until all the truffle mix has been used.

Clean your hands and then roll half of the balls in cacao powder and half in rose powder. You will end up with a mix of brown and pink truffle balls. Place the truffle balls in an airtight container in the fridge for at least 2 hours for the truffles to firm up before eating.

Truffles will keep in an airtight container in the fridge for up to 1 week (providing you don't eat them all).

Luffa

Luffa aegyptiaca

Luffas, also known as loofah or sponge gourds, are a type of vegetable that belongs to the cucumber family. Luffas are native to South and Southeast Asia, where they are grown as an edible vegetable and used in a similar way to squash or okra. The young fruit can be pickled like gherkins and the flowers are edible too. Luffas are also grown for their fibrous interior, which can be used as a natural alternative to synthetic sponges in the bathroom, kitchen and general cleaning.

- **Sow** spring
- **Aspect** full sun
- **Spacing** 50 cm (20 inches)
- **Height** 200 cm (6 ft 5 inches)
- **Frost & drought** drought tolerant, frost tender
- **Soil pH** 6.0–6.8
- **Part used** fruit
- **Preparation** food, sponge
- **Good for** lymphatic, musculoskeletal

Sow and grow

Scarify luffa seeds and soak them overnight prior to planting. Sow luffa seeds at a depth of 1.5 cm (5/8 inch). Shoots should appear in around 2 weeks.

Luffas like rich, well-drained soil. They require a trellis or climbing structure or they will sprawl along the ground.

They have a long growing season and will need a site that has 3–4 months of sunny, frost-free weather. If you live in a cooler climate, try growing them indoors in pots. Water at least once per week during the growing season. Avoid overwatering though, you just need to keep the soil moist, as luffas are susceptible to root rot.

To increase the chance of flower and fruit production, you can hand pollinate. Some people pinch off the first flush of flowers, as they believe the next flush grow better luffas.

Harvest

It will take 3–4 months of growth for luffas to be ready to harvest for their skeletons. When ready, they turn yellowish-brown and the skin feels dry and slightly brittle.

You'll need to soak the luffas in a bucket of water for a couple of hours to soften the skin. After soaking, the skin will pull off to reveal the fibrous interior. Remove all the seeds and let them dry, saving them for the following season's crop.

Hang the harvested luffa skeletons in a well-ventilated area until they dry completely. This usually takes a few weeks.

The harvested luffas will shrink and develop a rougher texture. Once dry, cut them up with a serrated knife to the desired size. Store in a cool, dry place until you're ready to use them – they'll keep for many years if dried correctly.

Luffa massage brush

Makes 1

In the bathroom, luffas make excellent exfoliators. Use them for dry brushing to help remove dead skin cells and dirt from all over your body, giving the skin a smooth appearance and healthy glow. It also helps increase circulation.

1 dried luffa
1 bamboo stick (optional)

✱ If using your luffa in the shower, let it completely dry out between uses, as leaving it in the shower increases the risk of bacterial growth.

Dry brushing is best done in the morning before you shower.

When first starting out dry brushing, or if you have sensitive skin, try brushing once per week and increase the frequency from there.

Use a firm pressure – but not so much that you scratch your skin. Use gentle pressure on areas of thinner skin, avoid the pubic area and broken or inflamed skin. You will notice a small amount of redness to your skin after brushing – this is normal.

Aim for 3–5 minutes of dry brushing using the following sequence:

- Starting on the soles of your feet, brush in small strokes moving from your toe to your heel. Give the thicker skin on your heels a good scrub.
- From the top of your feet move up your legs, using brush strokes that are always moving in an upwards direction towards your heart. Brush over each area with two or three strokes.
- Move to your knees. Use a firmer pressure on the fronts, as the skin is thicker and often needs a good scrub. Be careful and use gentle strokes behind your knees, as this is a sensitive area.
- Brush over the front and back of your thighs and hips. If you have sore hips, it may be nice to do broad circular strokes over the area, increasing the blood flow and offering pain relief.
- Gently move up around your torso – chest, back and shoulders. When brushing your belly, use strokes in a clockwise direction.
- Finish with your arms, using strokes that move from your hands to your shoulders.

Shake off your massage and then pop into the shower for a rinse.

After your shower, apply a herbal-infused oil or cream to moisturise and further massage yourself.

Perform dry brushing standing, or seated if you need support. If there are areas you can't reach, you can mount the luffa onto a bamboo stick so you can massage yourself.

Homegrown luffas are a little too harsh to use on your face or neck, so it's best to stick to your legs, arms and torso.

When your luffa becomes too old to use, simply pop it into your compost bin.

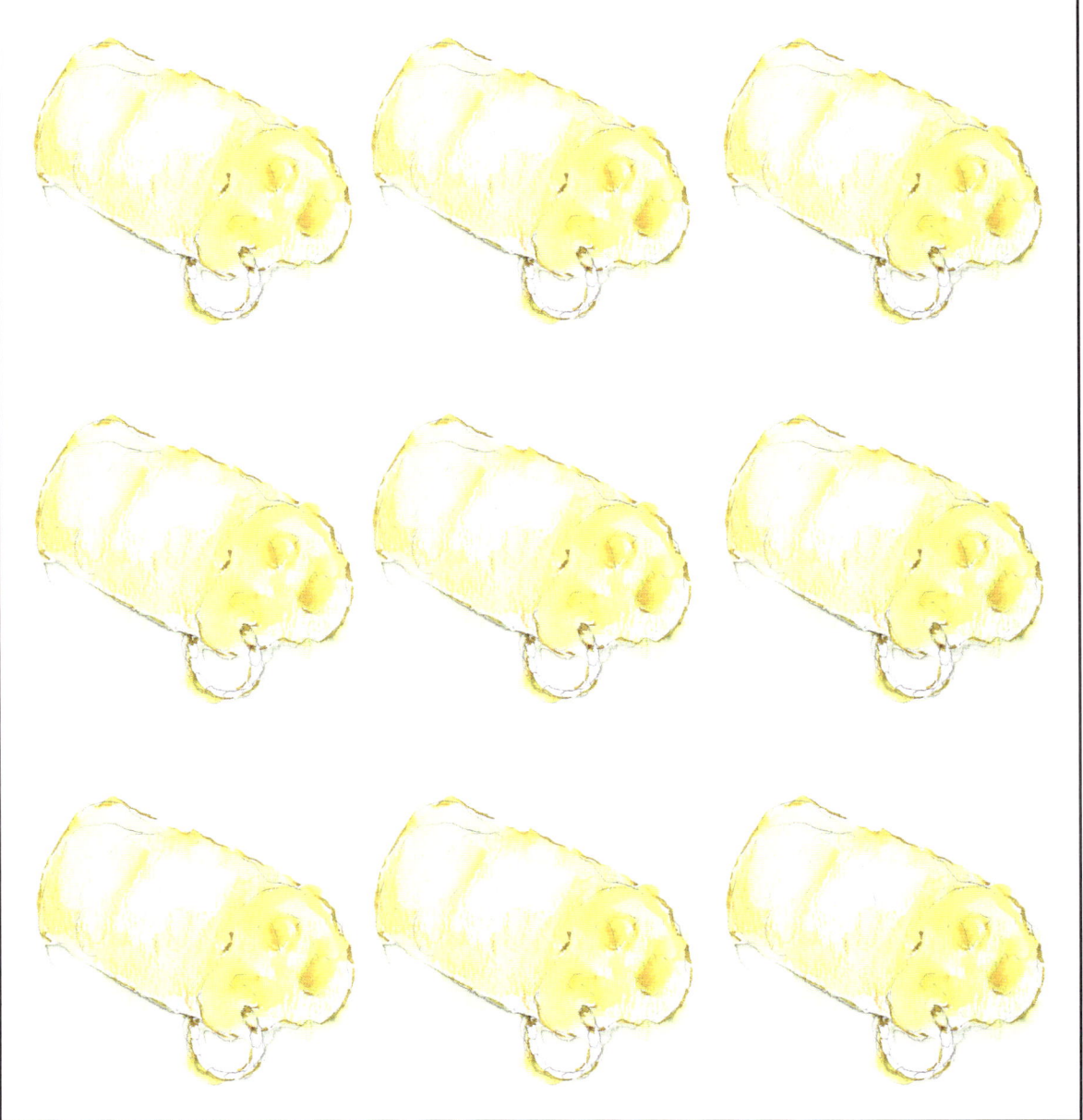

Plant profiles and recipes

Chamomile

Matricaria recutita

Chamomile flowers are well known to help ease nervous tension and aid sleep when taken in a cup of tea. A calming brew of chamomile tea can also settle the digestive system and help to relieve stomach cramps, bloating and flatulence. Make a compress or wash to cool down and gently soothe sunburn, rashes, bites and eczema. A cold compress placed over dry eyes can offer relief and may assist in easing the irritation of conjunctivitis. Chamomile's antiseptic and anti-inflammatory properties can make an effective gargle for inflamed, bleeding gums, help to heal painful mouth ulcers and soothe scratchy, sore throats.

- **Sow** autumn, summer
- **Aspect** full sun to partial shade
- **Spacing** 15–30 cm (6–12 inches)
- **Height** 60 cm (23 inches)
- **Frost & drought** frost tolerant
- **Soil pH** 5.6–7.5
- **Part used** flower
- **Preparation** compress, food, tea, tincture, wash
- **Good for** digestive, nervous, skin
- **Caution** known allergen

Sow and grow

Chamomile seeds are very small and can be hard to handle. Add the seeds to some fine sand to help scatter them and sow on the surface of the soil. Shoots should appear in 2 weeks.

Chamomile likes moist, well-drained soil that is rich in organic matter. Although chamomile likes cooler, moist conditions, overwatering will kill your plant. It hates getting wet feet. It will require some watering during dry spells.

Encourage abundant blooms by regularly deadheading.

Harvest

Chamomile flowers will be mature enough to harvest in around 9 weeks.

Harvest flowers that are fully opened by raking your fingers lightly through the blooms or pinch off at the base of the flower. Dry chamomile flowers as soon as you can after harvesting to retain their aromatic oils.

Chamomile flowers freeze well, retaining their oil content.

Store dried chamomile in an airtight container in a dark, dry place for 1–2 years. Keep frozen flowers in an airtight container for up to 6 months.

Chamomile, thyme and honey panna cotta

Serves 4

This beautifully aromatic panna cotta is super simple to make. You can play around with other herb combinations – elderflower and lemon, meadowsweet and orange, rose and cinnamon. The possibilities are endless.

If you are using panna cotta moulds, lightly grease them with vegetable oil. Alternatively, you can serve them in cute vintage glasses.

Place the milk, cream, sugar, honey, vanilla bean seeds, chamomile flowers and thyme in a medium saucepan over medium heat and slowly warm the milk, stirring, until just boiling. Remove from the heat and allow to steep for 10–15 minutes.

Strain the milk into a heatproof jug and discard the chamomile and vanilla.

Sprinkle the gelatine powder into the cold water and whisk to combine. Let it sit for 1 minute, then microwave in 20 second increments until melted. Add it to the warm mixture, stirring constantly until the gelatine has dissolved.

Pour the milk mixture evenly among the prepared moulds. Refrigerate for at least 4 hours until set.

Serve with a drizzle of honey and a sprinkle of chamomile flowers or thyme leaves.

The panna cotta will keep in the fridge for up to 3 days.

125 ml (4 fl oz) full-cream (whole) milk
500 ml (17 fl oz) pure cream
55 g (2 oz) caster sugar
1 tablespoon of honey (local if you can get it), plus extra to drizzle
1 vanilla pod, bean split lengthways and seeds scraped
10 g (¼ oz) dried chamomile flowers, plus 1 tablespoon more for serving
1 thyme sprig, plus 1 more for serving
1 teaspoon gelatine powder
1 tablespoon of cold water

Lemon balm

Melissa officinalis

Lemon balm has a gentle, soothing action on both the mind and the digestive system. A relaxing cup of lemon balm tea eases unsettled and jittery stomachs, especially when caused by nervous tension. Its mild antiviral and diaphoretic action helps the body sweat out a fever, making it a great home remedy for treating common colds. When applied topically, lemon balm can relieve the irritation and severity of cold sores. Crush up fresh leaves and rub them onto insect bites for instant relief. It also helps to keep annoying insects away.

- **Sow** spring
- **Aspect** full sun to partial shade
- **Spacing** 30–45 cm (12–18 inches)
- **Height** 60 cm (23 inches)
- **Frost & drought** drought tolerant, frost tolerant
- **Soil pH** 6.0–7.5
- **Part used** flower, leaf
- **Preparation** compress, food, tea, tincture, wash
- **Good for** digestive, nervous, skin

Sow and grow

Scarify lemon balm seeds by rubbing on medium grit sandpaper, then stratify in the fridge for around 2 weeks before sowing. Sow lemon balm seeds at a depth of 3 mm (⅛ inch). Shoots should appear in around 2 weeks.

Plant lemon balm where you don't mind it taking over – like many members of the mint family, it can get a bit weedy in the garden. It readily self-seeds, and is easy to propagate through cuttings, root division and layering.

Lemon balm likes moist, rich, well-drained soil. It likes water and a good feed of compost or weed tea during the growing season.

Lemon balm will die down in colder conditions. Give the whole plant a trim back in late autumn, and mulch over. Fresh new leaves will appear in early spring.

Pinch off the young growing tips to encourage bushy growth.

Harvest

Lemon balm should be ready to harvest in 8–10 weeks.

Harvest the leaves as you need during the growing season. Picking the leaves before flowering produces the most aromatic leaves.

If you are drying your lemon balm harvest, prepare them for drying as soon as possible.

Store dried lemon balm in an airtight container for up to 2 years.

Lemon balm, pea and zucchini fritters

Makes 16

These lovely, fresh fritters make a great lunch drizzled with the lemony yoghurt dressing. They're also a terrific, nourishing breakfast alongside poached eggs. Pop a few in school lunches or layer with your favourite fillings for an amazing veggie burger.

To stop the patties from being too sloppy, you'll need to squeeze excess moisture from the zucchini and silken tofu. Squish handfuls of the grated zucchini over a bowl to remove as much liquid as you can. Pop the zucchini aside into a large bowl. Next up, place the silken tofu in the middle of a clean tea towel (dish towel). Gather the edges of the tea towel around the tofu and wring out the excess liquid.

Scrape the tofu from the tea towel into a blender. Add in half of the peas along with the lemon balm, mint, garlic, lemon juice and zest. Blitz until lightly combined.

Scoop the tofu and pea mixture into the bowl of zucchini. Mix in the remaining peas, spring onions and 1 cup of chickpea flour. Mix until well combined. Add more flour if it seems too wet. Season to taste with sea salt and freshly ground black pepper.

Add 5 mm (¼ inch) of vegetable oil to a large frying pan and heat on medium–high. Once the oil is hot, dollop tablespoons of the mixture into the pan. Give each patty a gentle squish with a spatula and fry for around 4 minutes, until golden. Flip the patty over and cook for 2–3 minutes more, until golden. Set the cooked patties aside and repeat until all the mixture has been used.

Make the dressing by placing all ingredients in a blender and blitzing until smooth and creamy. Season to taste.

Serve the fritters with the yoghurt dressing for dipping.

The fritters and yoghurt dressing will keep for up to 3 days in an airtight container in the fridge.

Patties

1 zucchini (courgette), grated
300 g (10½ oz) silken tofu
235 g (8½ oz) fresh or frozen peas
10 g (¼ oz) lemon balm leaves
10 g (¼ oz) mint leaves
1 garlic clove, crushed
grated zest and juice of 1 lemon
2 spring onions (scallions), finely sliced
1 cup chickpea flour (besan), plus more if needed
vegetable oil, for shallow frying

Yoghurt dressing

3 tablespoons natural yoghurt
2 tablespoons hulled tahini
1 tablespoon extra-virgin olive oil
2 tablespoons finely chopped lemon balm
juice of 1 lemon

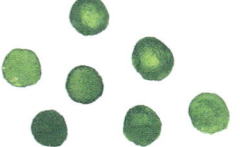

Peppermint

Mentha x piperita

Peppermint is extremely popular as a flavouring in toothpaste, mouthwash, shampoo, soap, food and drinks all across the world. If you head to the pharmacy you'll notice it as an ingredient in many over-the-counter medicines used for the relief of digestive discomfort – gas, bloating and upset tummies. The refreshing menthol aroma of peppermint is useful in steam inhalations, muscle rubs and headache balms. Topically, peppermint can be useful in fighting off fungal infections.

- **Sow** autumn, spring
- **Aspect** partial shade to full sun
- **Spacing** 30–45 cm (12–18 inches)
- **Height** 40 cm (16 inches)
- **Frost & drought** frost tolerant, mildly drought tolerant
- **Soil pH** 6.0–7.5
- **Part used** flower, leaf
- **Preparation** food, tea, tincture, wash
- **Good for** digestive, respiratory, skin
- **Caution** gastro-oesophageal reflux; avoid contact with undiluted essential oil on sensitive skin

Varieties

Mentha spicata – spearmint
Mentha suaveolens – apple mint
Mentha suaveolens 'Variegata' – pineapple mint
Mentha x gracilis – ginger mint
Mentha x piperita f. *citrata* – chocolate mint

Sow and grow

Peppermint is best grown from cuttings. You can also dig up and replant underground runners.

Peppermint likes well-drained soil, rich in organic matter. Flowers will bloom from summer through to autumn.

If you're growing a few varieties of mint, try to keep them in different parts of the garden as they have been known to cross pollinate. You may end up with new plants that have different characteristics to what you originally planted.

Harvest

Peppermint should be ready to harvest in 12–16 weeks.

Harvest the leaves just before the plant bursts into flower.

Store dried peppermint in an airtight container for up to 2 years.

Peppermint foot soak

Makes 2 cups, enough for 4 soaks

A refreshing foot soak for sore and tired feet.

Make small batches and store them in airtight containers as magnesium flakes can get a bit 'sweaty' when exposed to air. Alternatively, you can make a single-use soak using fresh plant ingredients instead of dried.

350 g (12½ oz) magnesium flakes
65 g (2¼ oz) sea salt
1 tablespoon baking powder
3 tablespoons dried peppermint
2 tablespoons dried rosemary
1 tablespoon dried lemon zest

Combine all the ingredients in a bowl and mix thoroughly. Transfer to an airtight container.

When you're ready for a foot bath, mix ½ cup of the bath salts with 250 ml (8½ fl oz) of boiling water in a heatproof bowl and briefly stir to dissolve. Allow to cool for 10 minutes.

Add the dissolved salts to a shallow basin or foot bath filled with warm water. Check the temperature is comfortable before popping your feet in and add some cool water if you need to.

Soak your feet for at least 20 minutes.

Bergamot

Monarda didyma

Bergamot supports the body through colds, helping to ease fevers and coughs as well as clearing congestion in the lungs and sinuses. Make an infused honey for a sore throat remedy or a steam inhalation with other aromatic herbs like oregano, thyme, sage and rosemary. Brew up a gentle, calming tea with lemon balm, catnip and peppermint for the nervous system. Bergamot eases general digestive complaints such as indigestion, bloating and nausea. Use a strong infusion as a topical wash or compress for abrasions and topical fungal infections. Bergamot is a popular culinary herb. It has a spicy, earthy, mint flavour with tones of oregano and thyme. The beautiful flowers make a striking addition to fruit salads, cordials and citrusy iced teas.

- **Sow** summer, spring
- **Aspect** full sun to partial shade
- **Spacing** 45–60 cm (13–23 inches)
- **Height** 100 cm (39 inches)
- **Frost & drought** drought tolerant, frost tolerant
- **Soil pH** 6.0–7.0
- **Part used** flower, leaf
- **Preparation** compress, food, steam inhalation, tea, tincture, wash
- **Good for** digestive, nervous, respiratory, skin
- **Caution** avoid medicinal use during pregnancy

Varieties
Monarda citriodora – lemon bergamot
Monarda fistulosa – wild bergamot

Sow and grow
Add the seeds to fine sand to help scatter them. The germination rate may benefit from seed stratification for 3–4 weeks before sowing. Sow seeds at a depth of 2 mm (1/16 inch). Shoots should appear in 3–4 weeks.

Bergamot loves rich, moist but well-drained soil.

It readily self-seeds and spreads runners throughout the garden.

It flowers in summer through to autumn. Prune spent flowers to encourage a second flush of flowers. Pinch off the growing tips every week or so to encourage a lush, bushy plant.

In colder climates, bergamot may die down over winter. When the plant starts to die back after cold weather or frost, prune it back to the ground, give it a feed and cover with mulch.

When watering, do so near the base of the plant, rather than the aerial part, to avoid powdery mildew.

The middle of mature bergamot plants can get a little straggly over time, so it's a good idea to divide the plant up every 2–3 years.

Harvest

Bergamot plants can be harvested from 10–12 weeks.

Harvest the flowers as they bloom and the leaves as required – the fresh growing tips are the tastiest.

Store dried bergamot in an airtight container in a dry, dark place for 1–2 years.

Bergamot and blood orange granita

Makes 650 ml (22 fl oz)

This pink-hued granita is a light and refreshing dessert for a hot summer's evening. Bergamot adds a punchy, herbaceous, minty flavour. Add a splash of Campari to the bergamot mixture for a delicious alcohol-infused granita.

2–3 teaspoons finely chopped bergamot leaves, plus extra to serve
grated zest and juice of 1 lemon
55 g (2 oz) castor sugar
500 ml (17 fl oz) blood orange juice (or the juice from five blood oranges)

Place the bergamot leaves, lemon zest, sugar and 125 ml (4 fl oz) of water into a small saucepan over medium heat and gently simmer, stirring until the sugar dissolves. Remove from the heat and set aside to further infuse for at least 1 hour.

Pour the blood orange and lemon juice into the cooled bergamot mixture and add a pinch of salt, to taste. Strain through a fine mesh sieve into a shallow baking dish and place in the freezer. Let the granita set for 1 hour, until the edges become frozen. Remove the dish from the freezer and use a fork to scrape in the frozen edges. Repeat every hour or so until the whole mixture is a frozen, shaved-ice consistency.

To serve, spoon the granita into pretty glasses and top with a pinch or two of finely chopped bergamot leaves.

You can substitute the blood orange for any citrus readily available, and the bergamot can be replaced by thyme, oregano, rosemary or basil.

Granita is best eaten on the day you make it. Leftover granita will keep for several days in an airtight container in the freezer. It may solidify, so remove from the freezer about half an hour before serving and freshen it up by scraping a fork through the mixture.

Catnip

Nepeta cataria

Catnip has a mild, gentle, relaxing effect on those suffering from nervous butterflies and stomach pains. A cup of fresh leaves brewed up with a spoonful of honey before going to bed can help to bring a calm and quiet sleep. Catnip may help to ease fevers when you have a cold. Brew some catnip tea or take a tincture for a calming and soothing remedy for stomach cramps and flatulence. In the garden, rub crushed up leaves on your arms to keep mozzies away.

- **Sow** summer, autumn, spring
- **Aspect** full sun
- **Spacing** 30–40 cm (12–16 inches)
- **Height** 150 cm (59 inches)
- **Frost & drought** drought tolerant, moderately frost tolerant
- **Soil pH** 6.0–7.5
- **Part used** flower, leaf
- **Preparation** food, steam inhalation, tea, tincture
- **Good for** digestive, nervous, respiratory
- **Caution** avoid during pregnancy

Sow and grow

Sow at a depth of 5 mm (¼ inch). Shoots should appear in 10–20 days.

Catnip grows in most soil types as long as they are well drained – it really doesn't like getting wet feet. It will appreciate a good shovel of compost in the soil. It also grows well in pots.

You can divide your mature catnip plants into a few clumps in autumn. Like all members of the mint family, catnip is easy to grow from softwood cuttings taken during the growing season in spring and summer. It roots in around 10 days. Catnip will also readily self-seed through the garden.

Deadhead flowers during the growing season for more prolific blooms. Cut back the old growth in autumn after flowering or wait until spring to cut it all down except for the new growth popping through the soil. Catnip can die down over winter.

Harvest

Catnip should be ready to harvest 2–3 months after planting.

Harvest leaves and flowers as needed during the growing season.

Store dried catnip in an airtight container in a dark, dry place for 1–2 years.

Tulsi

Ocimum tenuiflorum

Tulsi, commonly known as 'holy basil', is a sacred herb in India. It's a versatile herb with many health benefits. It can help support digestion; relieving cramping and bloating. It can ease the congestion of colds. A morning cup of tulsi tea can provide calming, soothing effects and it is believed to improve mental focus. Adding tulsi to your cooking imparts a bright, spicy flavour, reminiscent of clove, cinnamon and mint. Try adding tulsi to stir-fries, chutney, salads, green smoothies or a seasonal pesto.

- **Sow** summer, spring
- **Aspect** full sun to partial shade
- **Spacing** 30–45 cm (12–18 inches)
- **Height** 90 cm (35 inches)
- **Frost & drought** drought tolerant, frost tender
- **Soil pH** 6.0–7.5
- **Part used** flower, leaf
- **Preparation** food, steam inhalation, tea, tincture
- **Good for** cardiovascular, digestive, immune, nervous, respiratory, skin

Sow and grow

Tulsi grows well from cuttings, and a sunny windowsill is a great spot to keep them. The cuttings should take root in a few weeks.

Tulsi likes a moist, well-drained soil. It loves hot sunny weather. It will grow in cooler climates but it will die off in winter when frost strikes. In cooler climates, grow tulsi in pots. When the weather cools down, bring your tulsi plants indoors to avoid frost exposure. Give your plant a feed with compost or weed tea during the growing season.

To avoid tall, straggly plants, regularly cut the tips and flowers.

Harvest

Tulsi is ready to harvest in 14–16 weeks, or when the leaves are big enough to eat.

The optimal time to harvest tulsi is just before the plant is about to flower. Tulsi does well with small continuous harvesting, rather than one bigger harvest of the plant.

Fresh tulsi leaves can be blitzed up and frozen.

Store in dried tulsi in an airtight container for up to 2 years. Frozen tulsi will last up to 6 months stored in the freezer.

Chocolate and tulsi nice cream

Makes 550 ml (18½ fl oz)

This is a lovely dairy-free alternative to ice cream and it's super simple to whip up. Dried tulsi adds a refreshing hint of mint, cinnamon and clove spiciness to the classic banana and chocolate flavour.

Make use of overripe bananas for this recipe.

In a small saucepan over low heat, combine 250 ml (8½ fl oz) of the coconut cream, tulsi, cinnamon, vanilla, maple syrup and a pinch of salt and warm for 10–15 minutes, stirring occasionally. Remove from the heat and set aside to cool to room temperature.

Pop the slices of banana into the ice cube trays. Pour the infused coconut cream over the bananas. Place the ice cube trays into the freezer overnight, or for at least 5 hours, until frozen.

When the banana ice cubes are frozen, it's time to make the 'nice cream'. Blitz the dates, cacao powder, coconut oil and the remaining coconut cream in a blender. Stop the blender and add banana and coconut ice cubes on top of the mixture. Pulse on the lowest speed and slowly increase as the ice cubes break down. Blitz until the mixture is smooth and creamy – the texture will be somewhere between traditional ice cream and soft serve.

Serve in small bowls along with fresh berries and a sprinkle of cacao nibs for a bit of crunch. Finish with a dusting of ground cinnamon. If not serving straightaway, place the ice cream in an airtight container in the freezer for a couple of hours to firm up some more.

Keep leftovers in an airtight container in the freezer. It is best consumed within a week, but will keep for up to 3 months. Run through the blender to refresh the texture.

375 ml (12½ fl oz) coconut cream
1 tablespoon dried ground tulsi leaves
2 teaspoons ground cinnamon, plus extra for dusting
½ teaspoon vanilla extract
1 teaspoon maple syrup
2 very ripe, spotted bananas, peeled and finely sliced
2 pitted dates, roughly chopped
3 tablespoons cacao powder
1 tablespoon coconut oil, melted
fresh seasonal berries, for serving (optional)
cacao nibs, for serving

Oregano

Origanum vulgare

Besides being a popular culinary herb, oregano's antibacterial and antiviral properties make it a useful herb to help ease the symptoms of colds. It's great for breaking down phlegm and easing dry coughs. Make an infused honey drink or use it in a herbal steam inhalation. Use it as a mouthwash to treat irritated and inflamed gums, turn it into a spray for sore throats and use it as a compress on infected cuts and grazes. It makes a lovely bath with lavender and rosemary for skin infections. Oregano can help with the digestion of fatty foods, providing relief from indigestion, flatulence and cramping.

- **Sow** summer, spring
- **Aspect** full sun to partial sun
- **Spacing** 30–45 cm (12–18 inches)
- **Height** 60 cm (23 inches)
- **Frost & drought** drought tolerant, frost tolerant
- **Soil pH** 6.0–7.5
- **Part used** flower, leaf
- **Preparation** compress, food, tea, tincture, wash
- **Good for** digestive, respiratory
- **Caution** known allergen, avoid contact with undiluted essential oil on sensitive skin

Varieties
Origanum vulgare var. *aureum* – golden oregano
Origanum vulgare ssp. *hirtum* – Greek oregano

Sow and grow
Oregano is best grown from cuttings and root divisions taken in the spring and autumn.

It likes really well-drained soil, but it will cope with drier soil and little water. Don't overwater or over-fertilise your plants. Oregano that has grown in drier and sunnier conditions will be more aromatic. If you live in a cooler and wetter climate, try growing oregano in a pot with well-draining potting mix. Golden oregano (*Origanum vulgare aureum*) is a good variety to try out in cooler conditions.

Oregano grows well with other common Mediterranean kitchen herbs such as rosemary, thyme, sage and lavender. It's a good companion plant to all vegetables, especially those prone to aphids.

Give your oregano a good pruning back after flowering, even cutting the stems back to the ground. This will encourage new, bushy growth.

Harvest
Oregano is ready to harvest in around 12–14 weeks.

Harvest the leaves and flowers as you need. The leaves are best picked just before the plant flowers.

Store dried oregano in an airtight container for up to 2 years.

Oregano salsa verde

Makes 200 ml (7 fl oz)

This is delicious anytime, but especially good if you've got an upset tummy or fighting off a cold. The powerful antibacterial and antimicrobial action of garlic and oregano work together in this tasty salsa verde.

Use as an accompaniment to eggs and feta on sourdough for breakfast, stir it into Greek yoghurt for a zingy marinade, or use it as a dip for steamed globe artichokes for a tasty summer snack.

35 g (1¼ oz) oregano leaves, chopped
30 g (1 oz) flat-leaf parsley leaves, chopped
15 g (½ oz) mint leaves, chopped
1 teaspoon capers (or Pod pickles, see page 156)
2 large garlic cloves, crushed
4 spring onions (scallions), sliced
zest of ½ lemon
juice of 1 lemon
1 teaspoon caster sugar or honey
125 ml (4 fl oz) extra-virgin olive oil
2 tablespoons red wine vinegar
¼ teaspoon dried chilli flakes (optional)

Place all the ingredients in a food processor and blitz until a smooth consistency. Season with salt flakes and freshly ground black pepper, to taste.

Store the sauce in an airtight container in the fridge for up to 1 week or freeze in individual portions in ice cube trays for up to 6 months.

Parsley

Petroselinum crispum

Parsley is not only a wonderful culinary herb, it also has many medicinal attributes. It is a rich source of vitamin C, along with vitamins A and K. It also contains calcium, folate, iron, magnesium and potassium. Parsley can have a diuretic effect, increasing urination and reducing water retention and bloating. Parsley is also great for relieving stomach pains. A simple tea of fresh parsley leaves, peppermint, fennel seed and ginger is a lovely after-dinner drink if you have overindulged. Chewing parsley leaves can freshen breath. Rubbing parsley on your hands can help to remove the smell that lingers after chopping up garlic and onions.

- **Sow** autumn, spring
- **Aspect** full sun to partial shade
- **Spacing** 15–25 cm (6–10 inches)
- **Height** 60 cm (23 inches)
- **Frost & drought** drought tender, frost tolerant
- **Soil pH** 6.0–7.0
- **Part used** flower, leaf, root
- **Preparation** food, tea, tincture
- **Good for** digestive, reproductive, urinary
- **Caution** pregnancy, breastfeeding

Varieties
Petroselinum crispum var. *neapolitanum* – flat-leaf parsley

Sow and grow
Parsley seeds are notoriously slow at germinating but you can speed things up a little by soaking the seeds in warm water overnight. Sow at a depth of 3 mm (⅛ inch). The shoots should appear in 2–3 weeks.

Leave some of your parsley to self-seed and you will have a steady supply of plants popping up all over the place.

Parsley likes moist, rich, well-drained soil. When the weather gets too hot and dry, parsley is known for prematurely bolting to seed.

Parsley will go to seed in its second year. Cut back flower heads before they open and leaf growth should be extended for a little longer.

Harvest
Parsley should be ready to harvest in around 14–18 weeks from planting.

Harvest the leaves as you need them. Picking them regularly encourages young, tender growth. Harvest the roots during autumn or early winter in their second year of growth. Use the roots fresh like you would use parsnip or carrots in cooking.

Store dried parsley in an airtight container for up to 2 years.

Medicinal bone broth

Makes 1.5 litres (51 fl oz)

Bone broth is great for digestive health and gut healing, providing nutrients that make for strong and healthy hair, skin and nails. It makes a nourishing meal while recovering from illness.

Use bone broth as a base for soups, stews and risottos. A cup of bone broth with a squeeze of lemon and some fresh herbs makes a great snack on cold winter days.

To create a rich depth of flavour in the bone broth, I like to roast some of the ingredients beforehand.

....

Preheat the oven 170°C (340°F) fan-forced.

Place the chicken bones, carrot, celery, onions, garlic, parsley roots and mixed herbs on a baking tray and lightly drizzle with extra-virgin olive oil. Bake for an hour. Give everything a turn once or twice during cooking.

To make the bone broth, transfer the roasted ingredients into a large stock pot. Add the peppercorns, the remaining greens, calendula petals, bay leaves and apple cider vinegar. Cover the chicken and vegetables with around 3 litres (102 fl oz) of water. Bring to a boil and then turn down to a simmer, cooking without stirring for 8–12 hours.

Keep an eye on the liquid level, topping it up with water as you go, making sure the vegetables and bones are always covered. You want the liquid to reduce by about a third of the original amount.

If you have used a whole chicken or bones with meat on them, remove them from the pot after 2–3 hours so the meat doesn't disintegrate. Set the meat aside (you can use the meat in another dish or add it back into the broth if you are having a serve straight away).

At the end of cooking, strain the broth through a muslin-lined sieve. Compost the leftover solid ingredients.

Use the broth straight away or cool it and store it in an airtight container in the fridge for up to 5 days or the freezer for up to 12 months. For individual portions, freeze it into ice cube trays.

- 1 whole organic free-range chicken, leftover roast carcass, chicken feet or beef marrow bones
- 3 carrots, chopped
- 3 celery stalks with leafy tops, diced
- 2 brown onions, diced
- 1 garlic bulb, smashed
- 1 bunch of flat-leaf parsley using the leaves, stalks and roots
- 10 g (¼ oz) mixed herbs such as thyme, oregano and sage, roughly chopped
- extra-virgin olive oil, for drizzling
- 6–8 peppercorns
- 35 g (1¼ oz) nettle leaves, roughly chopped
- 20 g (¾ oz) dandelion greens, roughly chopped
- 5 g (⅛ oz) calendula petals
- 2 bay leaves
- 3 tablespoons raw apple cider vinegar or the juice of 2 lemons

Plantain

Plantaginaceae

Plantain's anti-inflammatory, antimicrobial and antiseptic properties make it a popular herbal remedy to assist in tissue repair and wound healing. Plantain can be infused in oil to make healing balms for small cuts, grazes and rashes. Use plantain externally on insect bites and stings or to help draw out a splinter.

- **Source** foraged, wild-grown
- **Part used** leaf, seed
- **Preparation** food, poultice, tea, tincture, wash
- **Good for** digestive, respiratory, skin
- **Caution** known allergen

Varieties
Plantago major – broad-leaf plantain
Plantago lanceolata – ribwort plantain or narrow-leaf plantain

A strong cup of plantain tea with a spoonful of honey can be used for dry coughs and soothing the irritated tissue of the digestive system.

The seeds from psyllium (*Plantago ovata*) are cultivated commercially to use in preparations made to feed and support the good bacteria in the gut, soothe the digestive tract and help keep you regular. The seeds and husks of the weedy varieties are also useful in this way.

Harvest
Gather the young leaves any time during the growing season. Pick leaves just before the flowers set.

Dried plantain leaves can sometimes have black patches. Despite the leaves feeling rather tough, these black patches are bruises from rough handling of the plant. A few black spots should be okay and not affect your infused oils too much. But discard if there is a lot of bruising.

You can dry the brown seeded heads by dry roasting them on a frying pan.

Store the dried seeds in an airtight container for up to 12 months and the dried leaves for up to 2 years.

Plantain seed crackers

Makes 20

These tasty gluten-free crackers are great dipped in some Chickweed pesto (page 141) or just munched by themselves. The whole seed head is used in this recipe.

Preheat the oven to 150°C (300°F) fan-forced. Line a baking tray with baking paper.

In a medium bowl, place the plantain, seeds, almond meal, rosemary and salt and mix well. Stir in the olive oil and boiling water until well combined. Place a plate over the bowl and let the mixture sit for 15 minutes.

Pour the seed mixture onto the baking tray, and smooth it out as thin and evenly as you can using a silicon spatula.

Bake for 30–40 minutes, until it has turned golden in colour and is hard to the touch.

Remove the tray from the oven and let the cracker cool completely.

Once cool, break the cracker up into the size you prefer.

Store in an airtight container for up to 2 weeks.

- 3 tablespoons dried plantain seeds and husks, ground up just before using
- 145 g (5 oz) mixed pepita and sunflower seeds
- 2 tablespoons sesame seeds
- 30 g (1 oz) flaxseeds, ground up just before using
- 25 g (1 oz) almond meal
- ½ teaspoon finely chopped rosemary leaves
- 1 teaspoon sea salt
- 1 tablespoon extra-virgin olive oil
- 250 ml (8½ fl oz) boiling water

Rose

Rosa spp.

A simple tea or tincture of rose petals can help ease digestive complaints. Rose can help alleviate the inflamed tissue of the respiratory system when we have a cold, acting as a decongestant. Rose petal tea or rose water used as a gargle soothes sore throats and may help to heal mouth ulcers. Rose petals can help red, hot, itchy, inflamed and irritated skin. Rose petals infused with witch hazel, elderflower and calendula makes for a cooling facial spritz and toner. Rosehips are known for their high vitamin C levels.

- **Sow** winter
- **Aspect** full sun to partial sun
- **Spacing** 90–120 cm (35–47 inches)
- **Height** 50–120 cm (20–47 inches)
- **Frost & drought** drought tolerant, frost tolerant
- **Soil pH** 6.0–7.0
- **Part used** flower, hips
- **Preparation** food, steam inhalation, tea, tincture, wash
- **Good for** cardiovascular, nervous, skin

Varieties

Rosa canina – dog rose
Rosa x damascena – damask rose
Rosa rugosa – Japanese rose
Rosa gallica – Gallic rose

Sow and grow

You're more likely to buy a potted plant or bare-rooted rose for your garden than to start them from seed.

Roses like well-drained soil, rich in organic matter. Roses are heavy feeders, so fertilise regularly during the growing season. Water the soil directly at the base of the plant to help prevent disease.

Some roses will only have one flush of flowers. For roses that rebloom, deadhead through the season to encourage new growth. Roses are generally pruned in late winter.

Harvest

Harvest rose petals late in the morning as the flower buds are just about to burst open. Gather rosehips when they have turned a bright orange-red. For a sweeter taste, harvest after the first light frost.

Dry the hips whole or halved on a drying rack in a warm, dry spot.

Store the rosehips and dried petals in airtight containers in a dry, dark place for up to 2 years. The petals will quickly fade when exposed to light.

Wild rosehip syrup

Makes 750 ml (25½ fl oz)

Pour this syrup into a tall glass filled with ice and top up with soda water for a special drink or drizzle it over Mandarin and rosemary cake (page 132) for a deliciously fragrant dessert.

Make this recipe your own by adding your favourite flavours. Orange zest, cardamom and cinnamon are all great flavours to play around with. You can also add rose petals to the syrup.

If you haven't grown the roses yourself, make sure the petals or rosehips you are using are pesticide-free. If you don't have access to homegrown roses, you could buy a packet of organic rose petal tea and use the contents of the teabag.

2 cups of fresh rosehips
220 g (8 oz) white (granulated) sugar
juice of 1 lemon
1–2 strips of lemon peel
1 vanilla pod, split and seeds scraped out

Give the fresh rosehips a good wash, trim off the stem and remove any dried up stamens from the tips. Roughly chop the rosehips, or quickly blitz them in a food processor.

Put the rosehips in a large saucepan with 1 litre (34 fl oz) of water and bring to a boil over medium–high heat. Continue boiling for 5 minutes, then turn the heat down to low and simmer for 40 minutes.

Remove from heat and let the liquid steep for 1–4 hours, or until the liquid has completely cooled.

Strain the liquid through a muslin-lined sieve. Gather the muslin into a bag shape and squeeze out as much excess liquid as possible.

Pour the liquid into a large saucepan and place it back on the stove, adding the sugar, lemon juice and peel, along with the whole vanilla pod and seeds.

Bring to a simmer, stirring, until the sugar dissolves and it becomes syrupy – around 5 minutes. Use tongs to remove the lemon peel and vanilla pod.

Pour the hot syrup into a hot, sterilised 750 ml (25½ fl oz) bottle. When the bottle has cooled, label with the date and ingredients.

Once opened, store the syrup in the fridge for up to 6 months.

Rose and oat face mask

Makes 80 ml (2½ fl oz), enough for 3 masks

This heavenly scented mask is really smoothing and hydrating. It's also great for your hands.

- 1 tablespoon dried rose petals
- 2 tablespoons oats
- 2 teaspoons kaolin clay (optional)
- 1 teaspoon natural yoghurt or the whey from your kefir ferment
- 1 teaspoon raw honey (local if you can get it)

Blitz the rose petals and oats into a fine powder using a food processor. Put the powder into a clean glass jar and add the clay, if using. Mix well. Store it until you're ready for a relaxing face mask

To whip up your face mask, place 1 tablespoon of premixed powder with the yoghurt, honey and 1 teaspoon of water in a small bowl and mix well. Add more water if needed. If it's too runny, let it sit for around 5 minutes to thicken up.

Apply the mask to your face using your fingers. Spread the mask over your face, under your chin and down the front of your neck.

Wait for 15 minutes for the mask to dry, then rinse it off with a soft flannel dipped in warm water.

Store the premixed rose and oat powder in an airtight container (labelled with the date and ingredients) in a dark place for up to 12 months.

Sage

Salvia officinalis

Sage is the herbal go-to sore throat remedy. It has long been used for the symptoms of laryngitis, tonsillitis and pharyngitis. Use a decoction of sage and thyme as a gargle or mouthwash to assist healing of inflamed gums, gingivitis and mouth ulcers. With its antibacterial, antifungal, antiseptic and anti-inflammatory properties, a compress of strong sage tea can be applied directly to minor skin conditions and wounds. Place a cool sage compress on the forehead or nape of the neck to help ease a headache. Brew into a tea with mint and lemon balm for a calming, refreshing cuppa.

- **Sow** spring
- **Aspect** full sun to partial sun
- **Spacing** 45–60 cm (18–23 inches)
- **Height** 60 cm (23 inches)
- **Frost & drought** drought tolerant, frost tolerant
- **Soil pH** 6.0–7.5
- **Part used** flower, leaf
- **Preparation** compress, food, steam inhalation, tea, tincture, wash
- **Good for** digestive, reproductive, respiratory
- **Caution** pregnancy, breastfeeding, avoid contact with undiluted essential oil on sensitive skin and long-term use

Sow and grow

Sage is best grown from cuttings or layering branches. Take cuttings in spring and autumn – place in a jar of water until little roots form then transplant to a pot or your garden in a spot with well-draining soil.

Once sage is established, it requires little watering and really doesn't like having wet roots. You can combat this by letting the soil dry out between watering.

Sage plants will become woody over time, pruning out old woody stems encourages new growth.

You will need to replace plants every 4 years or so for continued prolific growth.

Harvest

It takes 10–11 weeks for sage plants to be mature enough to harvest. Harvest lightly in the first year while the plant establishes itself.

Collect sage leaves before the plant flowers. Harvesting regularly during the growing season will encourage a nice healthy, bushy plant.

Rub the leaves off the stalks when the sage is fully dried.

Store dried sage in an airtight container for up to 2 years.

Sage deodorant

Makes 100 ml (3½ fl oz)

Sage and rosemary offer a herbaceous freshness to this homemade deodorant. The antibacterial and antiperspirant actions of both herbs work against the bacteria that cause unpleasant underarm odours.

This deodorant leaves your skin feeling soft and smooth.

....

Use a food processor to blitz the sage and rosemary to a very fine powder. Sift the powder through a fine mesh sieve to remove any larger pieces.

In a double boiler, melt the shea butter, coconut oil and cacao butter on medium–low heat. Remove from the heat and add the powdered herbs, arrowroot, kaolin clay and essential oil, if using. Stir it all together until it forms a smooth paste.

Transfer the paste to a sterilised jar and allow the mixture to cool and solidify completely before putting the lid on. Label with the date and ingredients.

To use, spoon out a pea-sized amount of deodorant from the jar and warm it between your fingers before applying it to your underarms. A little goes a long way. Apply once a day, or more frequently in hot weather or after exercise, as needed.

Store the deodorant in a cool, dry place for 6–12 months.

- 2 teaspoons dried sage
- 2 teaspoons dried rosemary
- 2 tablespoons shea butter
- 2 tablespoons coconut oil
- 1 tablespoon cacao butter
- 2 tablespoons arrowroot powder
- 1 tablespoon kaolin clay
- 5 drops of essential oil such as lavender, lemon, pine, spearmint, tea tree (optional)

Rosemary

Salvia rosmarinus

Rosemary is used worldwide as a culinary herb and it's believed to improve digestion, especially after fatty meals. Rosemary has long been used as a cure-all for hair health. It is thought to stimulate hair follicles, increasing hair growth. A hair rinse with rosemary will bring shine and lustre to dark hair. Massage rosemary-infused oil onto sore, tired muscles and joints to help increase circulation and reduce stiffness and pain. A steam inhalation of rosemary can help clear respiratory congestion and relieve headaches.

- **Sow** autumn, spring
- **Aspect** full sun to partial sun
- **Spacing** 60–90 cm (23–35 inches)
- **Height** 150 cm (59 inches)
- **Frost & drought** drought tolerant, frost tolerant
- **Soil pH** 6.0–7.5
- **Part used** flower, leaf
- **Preparation** food, steam inhalation, tea, tincture, wash
- **Good for** digestive, skin, musculoskeletal, respiratory
- **Caution** avoid contact with undiluted essential oil on sensitive skin

Varieties
previously *Rosmarinus officinalis*

Sow and grow
Rosemary is best grown from cuttings. Take cuttings from branches with fresh growth tips; these are the bits that are green and flexible. Place in a jar of water until little roots form then transplant to a pot or your garden.

Rosemary doesn't need too much fertiliser; lightly fertilise with fish emulsion or compost tea in spring. Tip-prune rosemary often for bushier growth. Give it a tidy up just after it has flowered – but don't cut back more than a quarter of the growth and make sure not to cut into old wood.

Harvest
Rosemary should be ready to harvest in 14–24 weeks from planting. Look for established plants that are putting on new tips and branches.

Harvest the leaves as you need; the most aromatic leaves are in summer just as the plant is about to flower. The fresh flowers make a pretty addition to your cooking.

Store dried rosemary in an airtight container for up to 2 years.

Mandarin and rosemary cake

Serves 8

The aroma from the kitchen when baking this cake is a heavenly combination of rosemary and citrus. The polenta and almond meal give the cake a moist crumb and the coconut sugar imparts a deep caramel flavour. This cake is perfect for sharing with those who have a gluten intolerance.

- 3 whole mandarins, plus 1 more, peeled and broken into segments, to serve
- 2 tablespoons fresh rosemary leaves, plus 1 teaspoon more, finely chopped, for sprinkling
- 100 g (3½ oz) coconut sugar
- 200 g (7 oz) unsalted butter, softened
- 3 eggs
- 200 g (7 oz) almond meal
- 150 g (5½ oz) polenta
- 2 teaspoons baking powder
- Wild rosehip syrup (page 124), to serve

Fill a medium saucepan two-thirds full of water and bring to a boil. Reduce the heat to low, then use tongs to carefully place three whole mandarins in the water. Simmer for around 1 hour, topping up the water as required – the mandarins should be covered with water.

Drain the mandarins and cool to room temperature. Puree the mandarins, skin and all, in a food processor until smooth. Put aside while you make the cake batter.

Preheat the oven to 160°C (320°F) fan-forced. Grease and line a 22 cm (8¾ inch) round springform cake pan.

Use a food processor to blitz the rosemary leaves or chop them as finely as you can.

Using a stand mixer fitted with the paddle attachment, beat the coconut sugar and butter until pale and creamy. Add the eggs, one at a time, beating after each addition.

Add the mandarin, almond meal, polenta and baking powder and beat on low speed until well combined.

Pour the cake batter into the prepared cake pan and bake in the oven for 40–50 minutes, until a skewer inserted into the middle of the cake comes out clean.

Let the cake cool in the pan for 15 minutes, then turn it out onto a baking rack. Carefully pull off the baking paper and let it cool completely.

Place on a serving plate and drizzle with Wild rosehip syrup. Decorate with slices of mandarin and a sprinkle of rosemary leaves.

Store leftovers in an airtight container in the fridge for up to 1 week.

Elder

Sambucus nigra

Elder trees have long been used in herbal medicines, and old English cookbooks are full of recipes for elderberry jams, jellies and wine.

- **Source** foraged, wild-grown
- **Part used** berry, flower, leaf (external use only)
- **Preparation** food, tea, tincture, wash
- **Good for** immune, respiratory, skin
- **Caution** avoid green and red berries; internal use of leaf may cause nausea and vomiting

Elderberries and elderflowers are most commonly used as a remedy for colds. Drinking a hot cup of tea brewed with the flowers is said to help fight fevers.

The leaves were traditionally used in external preparations for the relief of bruises, strains, sore muscles, burns, wounds and ulcers. They can also be used as an insect repellent. Simply crush the leaves to keep away mosquitoes and other flying insects.

Elderberries make a great dye. On this note, it's a good idea to use stainless steel or nonporous equipment for processing the berries.

Harvest
Harvest the leaves during the growth cycle. They are said to be more medicinal before the flowering stage.

Elderflowers can be harvested in spring and early summer when the blooms have fully opened.

Pick elderberries in late summer through to early autumn when they are dark purple, almost black in colour. Avoid any green berries and stems. Remove the berries from the stems by rolling them through your fingers, or you can use a fork to pull them off if you don't want purple-stained fingers.

Store the dried leaves, flowers and elderberries in an airtight container for up to 2 years. Frozen berries will keep for up to 12 months.

Spiced elderberry syrup

Makes 1 litre (34 fl oz)

Elderberry syrup is great to have on hand to help keep winter sneezes and sniffles at bay.

Have a play around with spices and flavours that you like – cardamom, nutmeg, ginger, licorice or star anise are some tasty options. Blackberries or rosehips are also a lovely addition.

....

Pop the elderberries, spices, ginger, orange zest and juice, lemon juice and filtered water in a large stainless steel saucepan.

Bring to a boil over medium–high heat until it reaches simmering point, then reduce the heat to low and gently simmer for 1 hour. Remove the pan from the heat, place a lid on top and leave to infuse for at least 5 hours, or overnight.

Prepare your syrup bottles by washing, rinsing and sterilising them in an oven.

Strain the berries through a fine mesh sieve over a large saucepan to catch the liquid. Use the back of a metal spoon to push the excess liquid out. Pop the spent berries in the compost or worm farm, or feed them to your chooks if you have some.

Add the sugar to the liquid in the pan and warm over a medium heat until the sugar dissolves.

Carefully pour the hot syrup through a funnel into hot, sterilised bottles and pop on the lids.

The syrup will last for up to 12 months.

- 500 g (1 lb 2 oz) fresh elderberries (or 250 g/9 oz dried)
- 1 cinnamon stick
- 2 cloves
- 2.5 cm (1 inch) piece of ginger, grated
- zest and juice of 1 large orange
- juice of 1 lemon or 1 teaspoon citric acid
- 500 ml (17 fl oz) filtered water
- 500 g (1 lb 2 oz) white (granulated) sugar or 875 g (1 lb 15 oz) honey (local if you can get it)

Elderberry gummies

Makes 24

Elderberry gummies have to be one of the tastiest cold and flu remedies around. They're quick and fun to make, and a great way to get kids into herbal medicine.

silicone moulds
1 tablespoon coconut oil, melted
250 ml (8½ fl oz) elderberry syrup
40 g (1½ oz) gelatine powder
125 ml (4 fl oz) hot water

Grease your moulds with coconut oil and sit them on a baking tray.

Pour 3 tablespoons of the syrup into a large heatproof jug and sprinkle the gelatine on the top. Let it sit for a few minutes to hydrate. Add the hot water to the gelatine mix and whisk until smooth. Add the rest of the syrup and whisk until well combined.

Carefully pour the mixture into the silicone moulds and pop in the fridge for 2 hours or until set. Remove the gummies from the moulds and store them in an airtight container in the fridge. They'll last for up to 3 weeks, if you don't eat them all straight away!

Elderflower fritters

Serves 4

This is a fairly common way to eat elderflowers in Europe. Despite being quite a simple recipe, these elderflower fritters feel special as there is only a small window of the year that you can eat them.

In a large bowl, whisk together the milk, egg and caster sugar. Whisk in the flour and cornflour, a little at a time, until there are no lumps. Add in the lemon zest and vanilla and combine well. Finally, whisk in the soda water, then set the mix aside in the fridge for 30 minutes.

Prepare a plate with paper towel for the flowers to drain on when fried.

Heat 5 cm (2 inches) of oil in a large frying pan to 180°C (360°F). You can check that it is hot enough by dropping a tiny bit of batter into the oil. The batter should float up and be surrounded by lots of tiny bubbles.

Hold the elderflowers by the stem and swipe them through the batter until fully coated. Let any excess batter drip off, then quickly pop them into the hot oil, flower head down. Fry for 1–2 minutes, until lightly golden and crispy. Place the fried flower heads on the paper towel to drain. Repeat until all the flowers are done.

Serve the elderflowers with some vanilla ice cream, a dusting of icing sugar and a drizzle of elderflower syrup.

70 ml (2¼ fl oz) cold full-cream (whole) milk
1 egg
2 teaspoons caster sugar
80 g (2¾ oz) self-raising flour, sifted
20 g (¾ oz) cornflour (cornstarch), sifted
1 teaspoon lemon zest
¼ teaspoon vanilla extract
70 ml (2¼ fl oz) cold soda water
vegetable oil for frying
12–16 fresh elderflower heads (choose large heads as they are easier to fry)
icing (confectioners') sugar, sifted, for dusting
elderflower syrup or runny honey for drizzling

Skullcap

Scutellaria lateriflora

Skullcap is commonly used in herbal remedies to improve sleep quality and calm busy minds. It also has mild pain-relieving properties. Its bitter flavour aids digestion and its antispasmodic properties can relieve stomach pains. Brew a cup of tea along with spearmint, lemon balm, ginger and cinnamon to help ease tension and relieve period pain.

- **Sow** winter, spring
- **Aspect** full sun to partial shade
- **Spacing** 30–45 cm (12–18 inches)
- **Height** 60 cm (23 inches)
- **Frost & drought** drought tolerant, frost tolerant
- **Soil pH** 6.0–7.5
- **Part used** flower, leaf
- **Preparation** food, tea, tincture
- **Good for** digestive, nervous, reproductive

Sow and grow

Stratify skullcap seeds for 1 month before sowing. Sow at a depth of 2 mm (1/16 inch). Shoots should appear in 3–4 weeks.

Skullcap will also easily grow from cuttings and root division. It spreads throughout the garden using running roots like mint.

It likes moist, well-drained soil that is rich in organic matter. Skullcap will tolerate sandy soil types as long as it is amended with plenty of organic matter.

Skullcap will die down over winter. Trim away any dead stems to encourage bushier growth when it sends up new shoots in spring. Deadhead spent blossoms in summer to encourage further blooming.

Harvest

Skullcap should be mature enough to harvest in around 17 weeks.

Collect the leaves of skullcap just before it bursts into flower.

Store dried skullcap in an airtight container for up to 2 years.

Chickweed

Stellaria media

Chickweed was traditionally used externally for wounds and itchy, irritable skin. You can make a compress using strong brewed tea, make a poultice from crushing the herb up, or make an infused oil using dried chickweed.

- **Source** foraged, wild-grown
- **Part used** flower, leaf
- **Preparation** compress, food, tincture, wash
- **Good for** digestive, skin
- **Caution** known allergen

Chickweed makes a great leafy green addition to your diet. It's high in protein and trace minerals, as well as vitamins A and C. Use chickweed as you would use any leafy green vegetable – raw in salads, chickpea pesto, juices and smoothies.

In the garden, chickweed is useful as a green manure crop. Chop it down and dig it back into the dirt where it will pop nutrients back into the soil in a much more absorbable form. Do this before the plant sets seed and it will help you to stay on top of its rampant self-seeding.

Harvest

Picking the leaves off one by one would take forever, so harvest the whole aerial parts of chickweed during the growing season. Chickweed is delicate enough that you can harvest it with a pair of kitchen scissors. Harvest the young tips on older plants, as they can become a bit tough and stringy.

The best way to preserve fresh chickweed is to freeze blended up leaves in ice cube trays. Store dried chickweed in an airtight container for up to 2 years.

Chickweed pesto

Makes 375 g (13 oz)

Chickweed pesto is the epitome of spring: fresh, bright and green. The taste is reminiscent of cucumber and cress. (Another pesto favourite is 'Nesto', made from nettles.)

The trick to pesto at any time is to keep a few staples in the pantry – this enables you to head out into the garden to gather seasonal leafy greens when you need.

To make a vegan version of this pesto, substitute the parmesan with 3–4 tablespoons of nutritional yeast. For a nut-free version, substitute the nuts for sunflower seeds or pepitas (pumpkin seeds).

3 cups of fresh chickweed, roughly chopped
2 tablespoons of pine nuts or cashews
2–3 large garlic cloves
50 g (1¾ oz) parmesan, grated
1 teaspoon lemon zest
1 tablespoon lemon juice
125 ml (4 fl oz) extra-virgin olive oil

Place all of the ingredients into a food processor and blitz until smooth. Season to taste with sea salt and freshly ground black pepper. Drizzle in a little more olive oil if the pesto is too thick.

Store the pesto in an airtight container in the fridge for up to 5 days. Drizzle a little olive oil over the top to reduce discolouration of the pesto. Pesto can also be frozen. Spoon it into ice cube trays and keep in the freezer for up to 6 months.

Comfrey

Symphytum officinale

Comfrey was used traditionally for speeding up the healing of broken bones, sprains, strains and bruises. It can help to provide relief for sore and swollen arthritic joints and assist with healing shallow cuts and grazes. Comfrey is also a great helper in the garden (see page 182).

- **Sow** autumn, spring
- **Aspect** full sun to partial shade
- **Spacing** 60–90 cm (23–35 inches)
- **Height** 120 cm (47 inches)
- **Frost & drought** drought tender, frost tolerant
- **Soil pH** 6.0–7.0
- **Part used** leaf, root
- **Preparation** compress, poultice
- **Good for** musculoskeletal
- **Caution** external preparations only, do not use for the treatment of deeper cuts and wounds

Sow and grow

You can grow comfrey by seed or purchase root pieces. Comfrey seeds do well with a period of cold before sowing, so stratify the seeds in the fridge for 30 days before planting at a depth of 5 mm (¼ inch). Shoots should appear in around 4 weeks.

Comfrey likes moist, well-drained soil with rich organic matter such as manure, compost and grass clippings.

If you need new plants, comfrey readily self-seeds. The easiest way to grow new plants is by root division. Any little pieces of comfrey root have the potential to sprout a new plant.

Cut comfrey back after flowering. Deadhead flowers for stronger leaf and root growth and to prevent the plant from self-seeding. Apply a good dose of fertiliser after harvesting leaves to help replenish growth.

In colder climates, comfrey will die down over winter, with lovely new shoots appearing in spring.

Harvest

Your comfrey plant should be ready to harvest after a full year of growth. If you need leaves before then, only harvest a small amount while the plant is busy developing its root system.

Once mature, harvest leaves as required, usually in warmer months and before flowering. Wear long sleeves and gloves when harvesting comfrey, as the leaves can be irritating to bare skin. Harvest the roots in spring and autumn.

Be patient when drying the roots – they should be crispy when dry.

Store dried comfrey in an airtight container in a dry, dark place for 1–2 years.

Comfrey leaf poultice

Makes 8–10

A comfrey poultice is a great home remedy to assist in reducing the swelling and pain of musculoskeletal injuries such as strains, sprains and bruises.

a bunch of fresh comfrey leaves and fresh roots
35 g (1¼ oz) plain (all-purpose) flour
10 cm (4 inch) squares of cotton cloth, such as old sheets

Blitz the comfrey and 250 ml (8½ fl oz) of water in a food processor until combined into a rough puree. (If you don't have fresh comfrey, dried comfrey works as well, but you may need a little more water to rehydrate the herb.)

Transfer the comfrey to a bowl and use a spatula to mix in the flour, a little at a time, until it becomes paste-like and spreadable.

Lay out a square of cloth on a cutting board. Place a spoonful of the comfrey mixture into the middle. Spread the mixture out to the edges, then lay another piece of cloth on top. Repeat to make more parcels until you've used up all of the mixture.

To use, place the poultice on the affected area and secure in place with a bandage or sports tape. Leave for at least 30 minutes, or overnight if possible. Repeat as needed.

You can store leftover poultices layered between baking paper inside a ziplock bag in the freezer. The poultice becomes like an ice pack, but with the added medicinal components of comfrey.

Fresh poultices will last up to 24 hours in the fridge. Frozen poultices will keep in the freezer for 6 months.

Don't use this poultice on broken skin or open wounds.

Feverfew

Tanacetum parthenium

Feverfew has traditionally been used as a remedy for headaches and migraines. Consuming 2–4 leaves every day is recommended to help keep headaches at bay. Feverfew should be taken regularly over several weeks before its effects are noticed. Feverfew can also be of benefit when pain and inflammation are present in conditions such as arthritis and painful periods. A wash of feverfew helps to repel insects as well as ease the irritation of insect bites. The bitter and pungent taste helps aid digestion and improves appetite.

- **Sow** autumn, spring
- **Aspect** full sun to partial shade
- **Spacing** 30–45 cm (12–18 inches)
- **Height** 100 cm (39 inches)
- **Frost & drought** frost and drought tolerant
- **Soil pH** 6.5–7.5
- **Part used** flower, leaf
- **Preparation** food, tea, tincture, wash
- **Good for** digestive, musculoskeletal, nervous
- **Caution** avoid during pregnancy

Sow and grow

Scatter feverfew seeds on the surface of the soil. Shoots should appear in 2 weeks.

Feverfew readily self-seeds. Feverfew can also be propagated by cuttings and root division in spring and autumn.

Feverfew will grow in most soil types as long as they are well drained. Depending on your climate, feverfew is a biennial or short-lived perennial. If you start seeds early enough, you'll get some blooms in its first year. During times of little rain, water the plants a couple of times per week. Give a feed of weed or compost tea and mulch in the spring.

Regularly deadhead spent blooms to keep the plant flowering. Pinch off the outermost set of leaves on each branch to encourage a bushier plant. Make sure not to trim off more than a third of the stem.

Harvest

The flowers of feverfew should be ready to harvest in 13–16 weeks.

Pick the leaves as needed, collecting them before the plant flowers. Feverfew leaves are best used fresh.

Store dried feverfew in an airtight container in a dry, dark place for 1–2 years.

Feverfew and spring greens frittata

Makes 12

Spring is a great time to make a herby frittata with an abundance of young, tasty greens, herbs and weeds ready for the picking. Feel free to use whatever you have growing abundantly in your garden. This recipe is super versatile – try adding tasty grated cheese, prosciutto or bacon. Or if you make this in summer, pop half a cherry tomato in the centre.

Feverfew has a rather strong flavour, start with a small amount and add more to taste. Make ahead for a great pack-and-go lunch.

5 small feverfew leaves
3–5 lemon balm leaves
10 small violet leaves
50 g (1¾ oz) baby spinach leaves
100 g (3½ oz) fresh herbs and greens, such as flat-leaf parsley, mint, dandelion leaves, mallow leaves, fennel, chickweed, nettles, chives, spring onion (scallions), rainbow chard
5 eggs
3 tablespoons pure cream
75 g (2¾ oz) Danish feta
calendula petals, to serve

Preheat the oven to 200°C (390°F) fan-forced. Lightly grease a 12-hole muffin pan.

Wash, dry and roughly chop the herbs and greens.

In a large bowl, whisk the eggs and cream together. Add in the herbs, along with a good pinch each of sea salt and freshly ground black pepper. Use a stick blender to blitz everything until it is bright green.

Fill the muffin holes three-quarters full with the mixture. Pop a little crumbled feta in the centre of each frittata.

Place the muffin pan in the oven and bake for 10 minutes, until the eggs have puffed up and the centres of the frittatas jiggle a little.

Serve warm or cold with a sprinkle of calendula petals on top.

Store in an airtight container in the fridge for up to 3 days.

Herb butter with feverfew

Makes 250 g (9 oz)

This is my take on a traditional way to consume feverfew. You can slice off portions of the butter as you need and spread it on fresh sourdough to make a tasty sandwich.

- 2–5 leaves of feverfew (start with a small amount and add more to your taste)
- 1 tablespoon chopped flat-leaf parsley leaves
- 1 tablespoon chopped mint leaves
- 1 tablespoon chopped garlic chives
- 1 teaspoon lemon zest
- 250 g (9 oz) unsalted butter, softened

Finely mince the herbs together and place them in a medium bowl.

Add the butter and lemon zest and mash it all together with a fork until well combined (you could also beat it in a stand mixer with a paddle attachment).

Season to taste with sea salt and freshly ground black pepper.

Place the butter onto a piece of baking paper and shape it into a log by rolling it in the paper. Cover completely with baking paper and pop it into the fridge to firm up.

This butter will keep in the fridge for up to 5 days, or you can keep it in an airtight container in the freezer for 3 months.

Dandelion

Taraxacum officinale

Dandelion was used traditionally as a spring tonic to detoxify the blood, improve kidney and liver function and clear wastes from the body.

- **Source** foraged, wild-grown
- **Part used** flower, leaf, root
- **Preparation** food, tea, tincture, wash
- **Good for** digestive, liver, skin, urinary
- **Caution** known allergen; gall bladder disease, gall stones

Dandelion is a great herb to help get your tastebuds adjusted to bitter tastes. Bitter foods can help improve digestive function and reduce uncomfortable digestive symptoms such as cramping, bloating and flatulence.

Use the fresh leaves in salads, cook them like green leafy vegetables, or make them into veggie chips like you would when using kale.

The blooms can be used for tea, vinegar, honey, infused vodka, wine making, jellies and cordial, fritters, baking and salads.

To make a tasty, warm beverage, roast the roots in a low, slow oven, or dry-fry. Powder the roasted root as you need it and percolate as you would coffee.

Harvest
Harvest the fresh, young leaves throughout the growing season. Leaves harvested in spring, before the plant goes to flower, are less bitter.

Gather dandelion flowers as soon as they pop out. If using fresh flowers, remove the stems and sepals as these can be very bitter.

Harvest dandelion roots after the flowers die down in autumn.

Store dried dandelion in an airtight container for up to 2 years.

Wild weed pie

Serves 4

This version of hortopita – *a traditional Greek pie made with greens – is made from seasonal weeds, herbs and greens gathered fresh from the garden.*

In additional to dandelion leaves, you could add any of the following to your weed pie: angled onion, broad-leaf plantain, broccoli leaves, chickweed, hairy bittercress, lemon balm, mallow leaves, nettle, oregano, parsley, rainbow chard, sage, sheep sorrel, spinach, thyme, young rib wort plantain and young yarrow fronds.

....

- 1 tablespoon extra-virgin olive oil
- 1 brown onion, finely chopped
- 1 leek, finely chopped
- 3 garlic cloves, finely chopped
- 4 cups of weeds, greens and herbs, chopped
- 4 eggs, lightly whisked
- 150 g (5½ oz) Greek feta, crumbled
- 500 g (1 lb 2 oz) ricotta
- 60 g (2 oz) cheddar, grated
- ¼ teaspoon ground nutmeg
- 2 teaspoons of lemon zest
- juice of ½ lemon
- 20 g (¾ oz) mint leaves, fennel fronds and calendula petals, chopped
- 125 g (4½ oz) salted butter, melted
- 12 sheets of filo pastry

Heat the olive oil in a large frying pan over medium heat then add the onion, leek and garlic. Fry until the onion is just translucent. Add the chopped greens and cook until they have completely wilted and softened up. Transfer to a large bowl and allow to cool.

Pour the eggs into the bowl with the cooked greens along with the cheese and nutmeg. Add the lemon zest and juice, mint, fennel fronds and calendula petals. Stir until roughly combined and season with sea salt and freshly ground black pepper.

Preheat the oven to 180°C (360°F) fan-forced. Brush a rectangular baking dish with melted butter.

Place a sheet of filo pastry on the base and sides and brush with melted butter. Repeat with five more sheets, brushing each sheet with butter. Pour the pie filling into the dish and spread evenly. Top with a sheet of filo, brush with butter and repeat with the rest of the sheets. Trim up any excess pastry and tuck the edges into the side of the dish. Brush the top with butter and use a sharp knife to score a diamond pattern in the pastry.

Bake for 45 minutes, until golden. Remove from the oven and let it cool slightly before serving.

Store leftovers in an airtight container in the fridge for up to 3 days. Freezes well for up to 6 months.

Thyme

Thymus vulgaris

The oil derived from thyme has strong antibacterial, antimicrobial and antiseptic properties, which makes it useful for destroying the germs that cause infections. Thyme can help to relieve bloating, cramping and gas, and is useful for aiding slow and sluggish digestion. A gargle of strong thyme tea relieves sore throats, as well as soothing irritating coughs. Common thyme (*Thymus vulgaris*) is the variety most often used as a medicinal herb, but other varieties still have some medicinal properties and culinary uses.

- **Sow** summer, spring
- **Aspect** full sun to partial sun
- **Spacing** 15–30 cm (6–12 inches)
- **Height** 30 cm (12 inches)
- **Frost & drought** drought tolerant, frost tolerant
- **Soil pH** 6.0–7.5
- **Part used** flower, leaf
- **Preparation** food, steam inhalation, tea, tincture, wash
- **Good for** digestive, respiratory
- **Caution** known allergen, avoid contact with undiluted essential oil on sensitive skin

Varieties
Thymus citriodorus – lemon thyme
Thymus citriodorus '*Variegata*' – variegated lemon thyme
Thymus herba-barona – caraway thyme

Sow and grow
Thyme is best grown from cuttings or root division.

Thyme originated in Mediterranean countries where it grows in poor, sandy, rocky soils. Plant thyme in well-draining soil that's not too rich in organic matter. Keep seedlings moist and protected from harsh sun until they are established. Let the soil dry out between watering.

Give thyme plants a good prune after flowering to encourage faster, bushier growth. Thyme is a prolific grower in summer, but in most climates it will grow year-round.

Harvest
Give your plants time to mature for 3–6 months before harvesting.

For the best flavour, collect thyme sprigs on a dry, sunny day when the plant is flowering.

Rub the leaves off the stalks when fully dried.

Store dried thyme in an airtight container for up to 2 years.

Nasturtium

Tropaeolum majus

Adding nasturtium to your diet has many health benefits. It contains carotenoids and high amounts of lutein, making it great for maintaining eye health. It's also rich in vitamin C. The antimicrobial and antibacterial properties of nasturtium can aid the treatment of fungal infections, especially of the hands and feet. Apply a poultice of crushed up leaves or a wash using the juice. The presence of sulphur-containing compounds in nasturtium make it beneficial for relieving symptoms of colds, such as congested sinuses. Pop a few leaves in your teapot, add some peppermint and ginger, and you've brewed up a tasty sinus-clearing tea.

- **Sow** autumn, spring
- **Aspect** full sun to partial shade
- **Spacing** 20–30 cm (8–12 inches)
- **Height** 30 cm (12 inches)
- **Frost & drought** drought tolerant, frost tender
- **Soil pH** 6.0–7.5
- **Part used** flower, leaf, seed pod
- **Preparation** compress, food, tincture, wash
- **Good for** digestive, respiratory, skin, urinary
- **Caution** avoid with peptic ulcer

Sow and grow

Sow the seeds at a depth of 1.5 cm (⅝ inch) so they can establish strong roots. Shoots should appear in around 2 weeks.

Nasturtium readily self-seeds. They do well in poorer quality soils, with richer soils encouraging foliage over flower growth. The foliage will trail along the ground, but can also grow up a trellis.

Established plants will need a regular water and feed during the growing and flowering season.

Encourage abundant blooms by regularly deadheading. Nasturtium will die down in extreme heat and cold, but due to their prolific self-seeding, new plants are never far away.

Harvest

Nasturtium should be ready to harvest in 10–12 weeks from planting.

Harvest leaves as you need when they are small and young. If you have an abundance of nasturtium leaves, you can even dry them to use as a peppery addition to savoury dishes or create a flavoured salt.

Gather the flowers as you need when they have just opened. Cut away the green base and stem if using for culinary purposes, as these parts can be a little bitter.

Pick the pods when they are about the size of a chickpea. Harvest green pods that easily separate as you handle them.

Pod pickles

Makes 250 ml (8½ fl oz)

Use these pickles in salads or in any dish in the place of capers. They are lovely paired with poached eggs and Chickweed pesto (page 141).

Fill a clean jar with the pods and cover them with water. Add in 1 teaspoon of salt per cup of water used. Let the pods soak overnight. Strain and rinse your pods, once again popping the pods back in the jar, covering them with water and adding in salt. Let them sit overnight. Strain and rinse again the next morning.

Don't worry if the pods smell a bit like rotten egg at this stage, nasturtiums contain sulphur compounds that cause this smell.

Pop the rinsed pods in a clean, sterilised jar.

Pour the vinegar into a small saucepan with the sugar, peppercorns, garlic, dill seeds and bay leaf. Bring to the boil. Take off the heat and pour the vinegar mixture over the pods. Leave on the bench to cool. Place the lid on and transfer to the fridge.

The pickles will keep in the fridge for up to 6 months.

150 g (5½ oz) nasturtium pods (or as many as you need to almost fill your jar)
250 ml (8½ fl oz) white wine vinegar
2 teaspoons white (granulated) sugar
5 black peppercorns
2 garlic cloves
1 teaspoon dill seeds
1 bay leaf

Nettle

Urtica spp

Nettles are known as nature's multivitamin. They are full of calcium, chlorophyll, potassium and vitamin C and dried nettles contain close to 40 per cent protein. They are great for increasing your resistance to hayfever, hives and allergies. A compress or brewed-tea wash can be a helpful remedy for urticaria, insect bites and stings.

- **Source** foraged, wild-grown
- **Part used** leaf, root, seed
- **Preparation** compress, food, tea, tincture, wash
- **Good for** musculoskeletal, respiratory, skin, urinary
- **Caution** known allergen; avoid contact with skin; internal overconsumption may cause urticaria (itchy skin)

Varieties

Urtica dioica – greater nettle, common nettle, stinging nettle
Urtica urens – dwarf nettle, burning nettle, lesser nettle
Urtica incisa – scrub nettle, native nettle

The nutrients found in nettles are not just good for the human body, they're good for the garden too. Use as a chop-and-drop compost or make up a weed tea fertiliser.

Try a brew of nettle, elderflower and green tea with a spoonful of local honey in the lead-up to hayfever season. Nettles are great for promoting healthy hair, skin and nails. Use a nettle-infused vinegar or strong herbal tea as a hair treatment after shampooing, leaving it on for 2–3 minutes before rinsing.

Nettle seed can be added to soups, stews, smoothies and baked treats for an extra hit of nutrition. Go easy, though, some people may find nettle seed over-stimulating.

Harvest

Harvest young, fresh leaves nettle leaves frequently through the growing season.

Blitz fresh leaves and freeze in ice cube trays for later use in your cooking.

Seeds are harvested in late summer and autumn. Push the seeds through a fine mesh sieve to remove the hairs.

Harvest nettle roots in late autumn after the plant has flowered. You'll find two layers of roots: shallow runners that make new plants, and a little deeper you'll find some thicker roots. Harvest the thicker roots and leave the thinner runners to start new plants.

Roots should snap, rather than bend when they are dry. Store the dried leaves, seeds and roots in an airtight container for up to 2 years.

Lemon and nettle cake with elderberry cream cheese icing

Serves 12

This vibrant green cake is a fun way to eat your weeds and greens! The cake is a light lemon flavour and the stinging nettles provide a matcha-like twist.

Preheat the oven to 170°C (340°F) fan-forced. Grease a 14 x 24 cm (5½ x 9½ inch) loaf pan and line it with baking paper.

Blanch the nettles by quickly dunking them in boiling water for a few seconds, drain, then rinse under cold water so they keep their bright colour. Lightly pat the nettles dry in a tea towel (dish towel).

Puree the nettles in a food processor or blender. This should yield around 1 cup of pureed nettles.

In a stand mixer fitted with the whisk attachment, whisk the egg yolks and caster sugar together until light and creamy. Drizzle in the olive oil, then the vanilla, pureed nettles, lemon juice and zest and whisk until well combined.

In a medium bowl, sift the dry ingredients together, then add to the nettle mix. Whisk until combined.

In another medium bowl, whisk the whites until soft peaks form. Add a heaped spoon of the egg white to the nettle mixture to lighten it, then add in the remaining egg whites, gently folding through.

Pour the cake batter into the cake pan and bake for around 30 minutes, or until the cake is lightly golden on top and a skewer inserted into the middle of the cake comes out clean.

Cool the cake in the pan for around 10 minutes, before inverting onto a wire rack to finish cooling.

Make the elderberry icing while the cake cools.

In a stand mixer fitted with the paddle attachment, beat the cream cheese, butter, elderberry syrup and 1 teaspoon of lemon juice on medium speed until smooth and creamy.

Turn the mixer down to low and gradually beat in the icing sugar until the icing is light and fluffy. Add in a little more elderberry syrup if you'd like a darker colour, and add more lemon juice if it's too sweet for your taste.

105–140 g (3½–5 oz) fresh nettle leaves
3 eggs, separated
345 g (12 oz) caster sugar
125 ml (4 fl oz) light olive oil
½ teaspoon vanilla extract
grated zest and juice of 1 lemon
300 g (10½ oz) plain (all-purpose) flour
3 teaspoons baking powder

Elderberry cream cheese icing
200 g (7 oz) cream cheese, softened
100 g (3½ oz) unsalted butter, softened
1 tablespoon Spiced elderberry syrup (page 135) or cordial (store-bought is fine)
juice of 1 lemon
100 g (3½ oz) icing (confectioners') sugar, sifted

Transfer the icing to a small bowl, cover, and place in the fridge for 30 minutes to firm up before icing the cooled cake.

Evenly apply the elderberry icing to the cake. Use fresh or dried herb flowers or a sprinkle of dried elderberries to decorate.

Store any leftover cake in an airtight container in the fridge for up to 5 days.

Nettle seed bites

Makes 10

These nutrient-packed balls make a wholesome and entirely moreish pick-me-up. Pack into school lunch boxes, enjoy as gardening and hiking snacks, or just enjoy one with your favourite cup of tea.

- 30 g (1 oz) nettle seeds
- 2 tablespoons dried nettle leaf
- 30 g (1 oz) flaxseeds
- 30 g (1 oz) sunflower seeds
- 15 g (½ oz) shredded coconut, plus 2 tablespoons more for rolling the balls
- 45 g (1½ oz) rolled oats (use almond meal for gluten-free version)
- 3 tablespoons cacao powder
- 1 teaspoon ground cinnamon
- 1 teaspoon ground ginger
- 125 g (4½ oz) nut butter
- 65 g (2 oz) hulled tahini
- 90 g (3 oz) honey (local if you can get it)
- 2 tablespoons coconut oil, melted

Use a food processor to grind the nettle seeds and leaf, flaxseeds, sunflower seed, shredded coconut and oats to a powder.

Pour the extra coconut into a small bowl. Line a baking tray with baking paper.

Place the ground seeds and the cacao, cinnamon and ginger into a medium bowl. Add the nut butter, tahini, honey and coconut oil and stir until it comes together like a dough. It should be easy to scoop the mixture into balls, but if it's too thick add in small amounts of coconut oil until it easily rolls into balls using your hands.

Roll the balls in the coconut until they are evenly coated and place on the tray. Pop the tray in the fridge for 30 minutes to firm up.

Store in an airtight container in the fridge for up to 5 days or in the freezer for up to 3 months.

Valerian

Valeriana officinalis

Valerian has long been used for its calming properties. It can be used to assist with anxiety, irritability and insomnia. Take a few drops of valerian root tincture in a warm cup of milk and honey to help induce sleep. The warming, bitter taste of valerian can help to ease digestive cramps. Valerian can also help relieve muscle tension, which may be helpful for period pain and headaches. Valerian makes a great companion plant, attracting beneficial pollinators to the garden. Pop the leaves into the compost; as they break down they add valuable minerals such as phosphorus, magnesium, potassium and zinc to the soil.

- **Sow** summer, spring
- **Aspect** full sun to partial shade
- **Spacing** 30–34 cm (12–13 inches)
- **Height** 150 cm (59 inches)
- **Frost & drought** drought tender, frost tolerant
- **Soil pH** 6.0–7.5
- **Part used** flower, root
- **Preparation** food, tea, tincture
- **Good for** musculoskeletal, nervous
- **Caution** may have stimulant or excitatory effect for some

Sow and grow

Sow valerian seeds on the surface of the soil. Shoots should appear in around 2 weeks.

Valerian readily self-seeds and it's also easy to propagate by division in spring and autumn.

Valerian likes moist, rich, well-drained soil. Mulch to retain the moisture in the soil over summer. Encourage abundant blooms by regularly deadheading. Remove the flower heads to promote further root growth. The plant will die down over winter but will shoot out new growth in spring.

Valerian can get quite tall, so keep an eye on it and use a stake for support if needs be. Valerian will grow in pots, but the pot should be big enough to accommodate the roots.

Harvest

Valerian flower should be ready to harvest in 15–17 weeks from planting. The roots will take longer to develop and should be ready after the second year.

While the valerian roots establish themselves, regularly cut the flowers off so the plant puts more energy into establishing roots. The flowers can be used to make tea, tincture and cordial. Harvest valerian roots during autumn or early spring.

Dry the roots until they are crispy and crunchy.

Store dried flowers and roots in an airtight container for up to 2 years.

Valerian spiced hot chocolate

Makes 500 ml (17 fl oz)

Valerian is well known for being a bit stinky, but this hot chocolate recipe masks the earthy muskiness of valerian root by combining it with cacao and chai spices.

Enjoy a mug to relax and wind down on a cold winter's evening, or if you've got period pain and need a little extra TLC, this is sure to hit the spot.

In a mortar and pestle, grind the valerian root, cardamom and cinnamon.

Place the spices, ginger, orange peel and milk in a small saucepan over low heat and warm for 5–10 minutes.

Strain the milk, then pour it back into the saucepan and add the chocolate and vanilla extract and stir until melted.

Once the milk is at your desired temperature, remove from the heat and stir in the honey, to taste.

Pour into mugs and serve with a dusting of cinnamon and some finely grated chocolate.

You can replace the fresh herbs and spices in this recipe with dried, ground ingredients and store it in an airtight container for a relaxing hot chocolate that's close at hand when you need it. It will last for up to 12 months in the pantry.

1 tablespoon dried valerian root
2 cardamom pods
1 stick of cinnamon
2 slices of fresh ginger
2 slices of orange peel
500 ml (17 fl oz) milk of your choice
2 large squares of dark chocolate, at least 80 per cent cacao
¼ teaspoon vanilla extract
1 teaspoon of honey (local if you can get it) or maple syrup
ground cinnamon, to serve
dark chocolate, finely grated, to serve

Mullein

Verbascum thapsus

Mullein is well known as a soothing remedy for inflamed and irritated tissue in the respiratory system, providing relief from coughs and breaking down mucous. The yellow flowers are collected and infused in oil as an earache remedy. Externally, the infused oil can be applied to assist in relieving the itching and inflammation of eczema, burns, wounds and rashes. Mullein root was traditionally used for relieving sore and stiff joints. A mullein root tincture can be taken for lower back spasms and pain brought about by overexertion.

- **Sow** autumn, spring
- **Aspect** full sun
- **Spacing** 30–45 cm (12–18 inches)
- **Height** 200 cm (79 inches)
- **Frost & drought** drought tolerant, frost tolerant
- **Soil pH** 6.0–7.5
- **Part used** flower, leaf, root
- **Preparation** food, infused oil, steam inhalation, tea, tincture
- **Good for** musculoskeletal, respiratory

Sow and grow

Stratify mullein seeds for 4 weeks before sowing. Add the seeds to some fine sand to help scatter them lightly on the surface of the soil. Shoots should appear in 2–4 weeks. Mullein can be slow to germinate (seeds can stay dormant for up to 100 years).

Mullein will grow in most soil types as long as they are well drained.

Mullein is a biennial plant, living for two, sometimes three years. In the first year, it collects energy, developing its root system and fluffy-leafed rosette. Then, in the second year, it uses up all of its energy shooting up a tall flower stalk, sets seed and dies.

Cut the tall flower spike back after flowering to halt self-seeding. Mullein is considered a weed in some regions.

Harvest

Mullein is ready to harvest in around 14 weeks.

Harvest the leaves in the first year and throughout the growing season as you need them. Check on the flowers daily and pick them individually as they open. Use the blooms fresh in salads, or collect them to dry.

Harvest mullein roots in autumn in their first year or spring for plants in their second year. The roots will easily snap in half when they are fully dried.

Store the dried leaves and roots in an airtight container for up to 2 years.

Mullein and garlic ear oil

Makes 125 ml (4 fl oz)

This is a quick remedy for when you have an earache coming on.

When using the leaves – fresh or dry – for any herbal preparation, make sure you strain them through a muslin-lined sieve to remove the fine irritating hairs.

2 large garlic cloves
½ cup extra-virgin olive or skincare sesame oil (available from health-food stores)
2–4 whole dried calendula flowers
1 teaspoon dried mullein flowers

Crush the whole, unpeeled garlic cloves with the palm of your hand and set aside for 5 minutes so the medicinal properties of the garlic increase.

Place the oil, garlic and dried flowers in a heatproof bowl set over a double boiler, gently warming on low heat for at least 30 minutes. If you need to use it straight away, scoop out a teaspoon of oil and let it cool down to body temperature before using.

Infuse the rest of the oil for a few hours if possible. When cool, strain and decant the oil into sterilised dropper bottle. Keep the bottle in the fridge and warm up the oil as needed. Discard the spent herbs in the compost.

To use, place one drop of oil that has been warmed to body temperature in each ear. You can gently massage behind and around the ears as well. Do this 2–3 times per day.

Do not use this remedy if there is a suspected ruptured eardrum, any discharge at all, or if there are tubes in the ear.

The oil will last in the fridge for 6–12 months. Gently warm before using.

Violet

Viola odorata

Violet can be used to soothe sore throats and ease coughs. Brew up a cup of violet leaf, plantain, thyme and honey tea for a soothing cuppa. An infused oil made from violet leaves and flowers can provide relief for dry skin and eczema. Rub violet leaves over insect bites for relief. The leaves and flowers of violets are edible, but the roots are not. The highly scented flowers make a beautiful purple cordial and an attractive decoration to baked goods. Use violet leaves like you would rocket (arugula), baby spinach leaves and basil. Toss it through scrambled eggs or add it to stir-fries, soups and stews.

- **Sow** autumn, spring
- **Aspect** partial shade to full shade
- **Spacing** 15–20 cm (6–8 inches)
- **Height** 30 cm (12 inches)
- **Frost & drought** drought tender, frost tolerant
- **Soil pH** 6.0–7.0
- **Part used** flower, leaf
- **Preparation** food, tea, tincture, wash
- **Good for** lymphatic, respiratory, skin

Sow and grow

The easiest way to grow violets is by division of their underground rhizomes and planting up their prolific runners.

Violets enjoy moist, well-drained soils. If your violets are growing in a sunny spot, they may need a good drink of water on hot summer days.

Go through your violet patch every couple of seasons and pull out the more mature plants, so that the rooted runners can get a chance to establish and produce more prolific flowers.

Violet has two kinds of flowers: the upright, scented, above-ground flowers, and cleistogamous flowers, which grow underground and are self-fertile. The cleistogamous (closed) flowers are not edible.

Harvest

Violet plants should be big enough for small harvests after 3 months.

Harvest the flowers as they open up. When harvesting the leaves, choose the smaller, younger leaves as they are tastier.

Store dried flowers and leaves in an airtight container for up to 2 years.

Garden greens dip

Makes 850 g (1 lb 4 oz)

This vibrant green dip makes use of an abundance of spring greens and herbs from the garden. Violet leaves add a peppery touch, similar to cress or young rocket (arugula) leaves. Use what you have readily available and enjoy changing up the ingredients as the seasons change.

Place all of the ingredients into a food processor with a pinch of salt and pulse until it is just combined. You may need to scrape the sides down and blitz some more until the dip is your preferred consistency. If the hummus is too thick, add a little warm water; if it's too thin, add a little more tahini.

Transfer to a bowl, drizzle with extra-virgin olive oil and serve with Plantain seed crackers (page 121), toasted pita, veggie sticks, or use it as a sandwich spread.

The dip will keep in the fridge in an airtight container for up to 3 days.

- handful of young violet leaves
- 35 g (1 oz) seasonal greens and herbs from the garden such as dandelion leaf, flat-leaf parsley, mint, lemon balm, chickweed, gotu kola, roughly chopped
- 525 g (1 lb 3 oz) young broad beans, podded, or 1 x 400 g (14 oz) can chickpeas or cannellini beans
- ½ avocado, roughly chopped
- 1 garlic clove, crushed
- 2 tablespoons hulled tahini
- juice of 1 lime
- 2 tablespoons extra-virgin olive oil, plus extra to drizzle

Plant profiles and recipes

Ginger

Zingiber officinale

Ginger is well known for relieving motion sickness. A cup of ginger tea can ease bloating, cramping and flatulence. Ginger can be great for improving circulation. Brew a strong infusion of ginger and peppermint for a warming, stimulating foot soak. A warm compress of freshly grated ginger may provide relief to swollen, painful joints. It is also a handy kitchen remedy for colds, working as a natural decongestant, helping to break down mucus and relieve respiratory and sinus infections. Gargle with a strong ginger and thyme infusion for sore throats or coughs.

- **Sow** spring
- **Aspect** full sun to partial sun
- **Spacing** 20–30 cm (8–12 inches)
- **Height** 100 cm (39 inches)
- **Frost & drought** frost tender
- **Soil pH** 5.5–7.0
- **Part used** rhizome
- **Preparation** compress, food, tea, tincture
- **Good for** circulatory, digestive, musculoskeletal, respiratory
- **Caution** gallstones, peptic ulcer, pregnancy, taking warfarin

Sow and grow

Plant ginger from divided rhizomes with the growing nodules facing up. The soil should just cover the rhizomes. Cover the soil with a plastic bag or a cloche to act as a mini greenhouse, trapping in warmth and humidity. Remove the cloche when shoots appear in around 4 weeks.

Ginger likes moist, well-drained, loamy soil types rich in organic matter. It doesn't like wet feet or cold wind.

In cooler and frost-prone climates, grow ginger in a greenhouse or in pots that you can move around. Plants go dormant in colder months. (You can dig ginger plants up and store them away over winter like you would for dahlias.)

Harvest

Ginger plants should be mature enough for harvest 10–12 months after planting.

Harvest ginger roots in autumn when the stems and flowers have died down. The longer you leave ginger in the ground, the spicier and hotter the taste will be.

Cut the stems 1–2 cm (½–¾ inches) from the top of the rhizome. Store fresh ginger at room temperature or in the fridge. Leave the skin on until you are ready to use it. For longer term storage, grate the ginger and store it in the freezer.

You can store the dried ginger in an airtight container for up to 2 years. Grind into a powder as needed. Store fresh, frozen ginger in the freezer for up to 6 months.

Ginger and lemongrass lozenges

Makes 40

These delicious lozenges are great for nausea and upset tummies, or as a sweet treat.

....

Place the ginger, lemongrass and peppermint in a medium saucepan. Pour enough water to cover the herbs by 2–3 cm (1 inch). Pop a lid on the saucepan and bring to a boil over medium heat, then reduce the heat to low and simmer for 15 minutes. Keep an eye on the water level and add a little more if needed.

Prepare candy moulds by brushing them with light olive oil or melted coconut oil or line a baking tray with baking paper.

Once your herbs are infused, strain and measure out 250 ml (8½ fl oz) of liquid. Compost the spent herbs or re-use to make yourself a nice cuppa. Pour the measured liquid back into the saucepan and add the honey and sugar. Heat on medium–high and stir for 5 minutes, until the sugar is dissolved. Place a sugar thermometer into the liquid to keep an eye on the temperature as it comes to a boil. Don't stir your mixture at this point. As it boils, use a damp pastry brush to brush down the sides of the pan to remove the crystalised sugar. You want the temperature to reach 140°C (285°F) for chewy lozenges – this could take up to 25 minutes. As always when boiling sugar, please take extra care.

Carefully spoon or pour the mixture into your moulds, or drop little circles of mixture onto the lined baking tray. Let the lozenges cool and set overnight.

Dust the lozenges in a small bowl with the icing sugar and arrowroot. Get rid of excess icing sugar by shaking the lozenges in a fine mesh sieve.

Once dusted, store the lozenges in an airtight container, using baking paper between any layers, for up to 4 weeks.

- 100 g (3½ oz) fresh ginger, peeled and grated
- 3 tablespoons ground dried ginger
- 3 stalks lemongrass, roughly chopped, bottom third of stem only
- 15 g (½ oz) dried peppermint leaves
- 1 tablespoon honey (local if you can get it)
- 220 g (8 oz) white (granulated) sugar
- 2 teaspoons each of icing (confectioners') sugar and arrowroot, sifted, for dusting

Chapter 02

All about your herb garden

Growing medicinal plants

Bed preparation

Choose a sunny spot in the garden to plant your herbs. Somewhere that gets about half a day of direct sunlight and where the soil is moist, free-draining and has been worked through with plenty of organic matter. There are always exceptions to the conditions herbs like, so check up on your chosen herb to find the right spot in your garden.

GREENS are rich in nitrogen and will decompose quickly. They include materials such as kitchen scraps, coffee grounds, fresh plant prunings, grass clippings, a layer of comfrey leaves and well-rotted animal manure.

BROWNS are rich in carbon and break down slowly. They include materials such as straw, dry leaves, newspaper, wood chips and sawdust from untreated wood.

Making a lasagne bed

A great way to make a herb bed from scratch is to make a lasagne bed. Composed of layers of cardboard, compost and mulch, this type of bed is used to help build healthy soils and smother weeds, and it involves little to no digging. It also makes great use of recycled materials.

Collect newspaper and cardboard and remove any sticky tape or plastic labels.

Mark out the size of the garden bed you want. (You can start lasagne beds in existing gardens and raised beds too.)

Start the first layer with cardboard. Overlap the edges and give the cardboard a soak with the hose.

For the next few layers, alternate greens and browns. The brown layers should be about twice the height of the green layers. Give each layer a good water as you go.

Finish the last two layers with compost and a generous topping of mulch such as pea straw mulch, sugar cane mulch, wood chips or lucerne. The depth of your lasagne bed should be around 30–60 cm (12–23 inches) to begin with, this will reduce over time as everything breaks down.

The bed will be ready to plant within a few weeks to a few months, depending on the weather conditions.

If you want to plant into your lasagne bed before it starts to break down, make the top compost layer around 10 cm (4 inches) thick. Plant directly into the compost, then mulch around the plants. Use annuals with shallower roots to begin with such as, chamomile, California poppy or nasturtium.

Compost	Mulch
Compost improves and enriches the soil quality and structure, increases moisture retention, balances the soil pH and provides nutrients for your herbs. Making your own compost is a fantastic way to make use of food scraps and to recycle garden waste. To start your compost, find a place for your compost heap or bin that is accessible to both your house and the garden. It should be in a free-draining spot, where it will get some sunlight, but not in full sun. To make your compost, you'll need a mix of greens and browns at a ratio of one part greens to three parts browns. Place the greens and browns in alternating layers in your heap. Make sure larger materials are chopped, shredded or mulched down to speed up their decomposition. Turn your compost regularly using a garden fork or shovel. This aerates the compost, helping everything break down faster. Compost bin tumblers are a great option for giving your compost a good mix without hurting your back. Keep your compost heap fairly moist. If you hold some in your hand and squeeze it, it should be damp but not sopping wet. Give the compost some more greens and a little water if it's too dry and add more browns, such as dried leaf matter or shredded paper, if it's too wet. It will take a few months for everything to break down. Chamomile, comfrey, dandelion, nettles, valerian flowers and yarrow can be added to your compost to help speed things up. If you don't have the space for a compost heap, try out a bokashi bin. A bokashi is a little bucket that sits on your kitchen bench and ferments food scraps into a nutrient-rich soil conditioner that you can dig back into the garden.	Mulching protects soil from drying out in hot, dry and windy conditions, or washing away in torrential rain. A good layer of mulch can reduce water evaporation by almost 70 per cent. Mulch acts as an insulator to the soil, regulating soil temperature and protecting roots from heat and cold. Over time, mulch breaks down, improving the soil structure and moisture retention. Mulch is great for slowing down weeds. You can suppress weeds and prevent their seeds from growing by mulching with newspaper and pea straw. Give the bed a quick weed if needed, lay newspaper on top, wet down with the hose and then cover with a thick layer of mulch. Make sure your mulch is free from weed seeds – sugar cane mulch and wood chips are good weed-free options. There are many different types of mulching materials and techniques. Choose what is readily available and affordable for you: - **comfrey leaves and other chopped up herb trimmings** - **fallen autumn leaves** - **lucerne** - **pea straw** - **sheet mulching** - **sugar cane mulch** - **wood chips and bark left to sit for a few weeks** - **woodier trimmings run through a garden mulcher.**

Herbs in containers

Most herbs will grow well in pots. Pots will fit on balconies, verandas, courtyards and the tiniest of spaces. Some people like to have pots of culinary herbs near the back door so they can duck out for a snip of herbs when cooking dinner.

A few pots sitting together on a balcony will create their own little microclimate. They're easy to move around to cater to changing weather conditions. When the summer sun gets too blistering hot or winter frosts are on the way, you can move the pot to a more suitable or sheltered position.

Pop a little gravel in the bottom of the pot and always use a good quality potting mix that is well draining. Add some agricultural sand to the mix for sun-loving Mediterranean herbs.

Mulch the pots so they don't dry out too quickly. Give pots a water whenever the top 2 cm (¾ inch) is feeling dry. Water the soil at the base of the plant rather than the leaves to help prevent diseases. In wetter climates or during winter, check that the soil is draining well, and the plants haven't become waterlogged or the roots haven't started to rot.

Your plants will tell you if they like how and where you've planted them.

Fertilise your pots while the plants are actively growing and flowering. Use a weed or compost tea, seaweed solution or even pop in a comfrey leaf to break down in the pot.

The more you harvest the leaves and flowers, the more your plant will grow and develop into a nice bushy shape.

You can have one plant per pot or a few herbs together, especially if they have similar growing conditions like the Mediterranean kitchen herbs – thyme, sage, oregano and rosemary. You can also grow two herbs of differing heights in a pot – for example, some thyme under a bay tree.

Growing a potted tea garden

There's nothing like heading outside to pick a few leaves and beautiful blooms from fragrant herbs to brew up a tasty morning cup of tea.

Planting a tea garden is a fantastic way for kids to learn about gardening, as well as being an introduction to medicinal herbs.

Whatever you decide to plant your herbs in, be sure to use a moist, but well-drained potting mix. Water your seeds and seedlings in with some weed or compost tea. Let the top few centimetres of soil dry out between watering as most herbs don't like getting soggy roots.

During the growing season, your potted herbs may like an extra feed of fertiliser or weed tea. As they grow, pinch off the young tips to use in tea – this also encourages a bushier plant. Pick flowers as they open to encourage a second flush of blooms.

Use the herbs fresh, or dry them out so you have tea on hand during the dormant months.

You will need

a variety of pots including repurposed and found objects such as old teapots and teacups, with drainage holes

10 HERBS FOR A POTTED TEA GARDEN

A mix of vibrant flowers, flavours and leaf shapes for a pretty collection and the perfect cup of garden tea:

- Anise hyssop (page 15)
- Bergamot (page 102)
- Calendula (page 36)
- Chamomile (page 93)
- Echinacea (page 54)
- Lemon balm (page 96)
- Peppermint (page 100)
- Sage (page 127)
- Thyme (page 152)
- Tulsi (page 109)

Herbs for garden care

Herbs not only provide medicine, but their beneficial properties can be of use in the garden.

Chamomile

Chamomile tea is a natural fungicide for the garden. A strong brew of chamomile tea can be used to spray seedlings to prevent conditions like damping off, which is a fungal disease that thrives in damp, cool conditions and appears as a fuzzy white growth on your seedlings.

See also page 93.

Comfrey

Comfrey has a deep-reaching taproot that can break up clay soil, providing aeration for the soil, increasing water drainage and bringing nutrients up into the topsoil.

Comfrey makes a wonderful weed tea (page 185) because of the nutrient-rich goodness it draws up from the soil. When you add comfrey tea to your compost or spray it onto your garden beds, it provides nature's most important nutrients – nitrogen, phosphorus and potassium. Comfrey tea benefits overall plant growth and encourages prolific flowering and fruiting. Use comfrey leaves as a mulch. Cut the leaves and place them around the edges of plants, or dig them into the soil and pop some mulch on the top. Plant comfrey in its own garden bed, as any disruption of its roots will sprout forth a new plant and it can easily become weedy in your garden.

See also page 142.

Dandelion

Dandelions grow a deep taproot that aerates the soil, loosening up impacted and heavy ground and improving water drainage. You can put whole dandelions into the compost to speed up its decomposition and add a multitude of minerals back into the soil. Add the whole plant into weed tea.

See also page 148.

Nettle

The older growth from nettles is ideal to make into a weed tea (keep the tasty, new growth for food and medicine), and if you have an abundance, go right ahead and use the whole plant including the roots. Make sure to use nettles before they go to seed so you don't accidentally spread them everywhere.

The high nitrogen content of nettles makes them a great compost activator. You can pour nettle weed tea and discard spent plants into your compost to help speed things up. Use nettle weed tea as a foliar feed or spray on plants to deter pests.

See also page 159.

Valerian	Yarrow
Valerian flowers are used in biodynamic preparations. Add them to your compost to speed up its decomposition. A fermented valerian tea can be sprayed onto plants just before flowering to encourage abundant blooms and a fine spray misted on plants the evening before an expected frost will prevent frost damage. The beautiful blooms also bring plenty of beneficial pollinators to your garden. See also page 162.	Yarrow can be used as an insect repellent and added to the compost as an accelerator to speed up decomposition and put nutrients back into the soil. Brew a herbal tea to spray onto sick plants. See also page 12.

Weeds

What are weeds exactly? It really depends on who you ask. If you ask a herbalist or anyone interested in permaculture, they will rattle off the beneficial uses of weeds for food, medicine, pest control, soil health, biodiversity – you get the picture. There are times, however, when you will need to remove weeds so they don't strangle and out-compete the other plants in the garden.

Weed management

The best time to tackle weeds is when they are young. Lightly run a hoe across the top of the soil, cutting the little sprouted weeds at the root. Leave the pulled weeds on top of the soil and let the sun cook them, then dig them back into the soil for a nutrient boost. If you don't have time to pull whole weeds out, simply snip off flower heads before they have a chance to seed into the garden. Keeping on top of deadheading herbs that readily self-seed can also prevent them from becoming weedy in the garden.

Use sheet mulch early in the season to help suppress weeds.

Nature always tries to cover over bare soil, so try to arrange the planting in your garden so there aren't many empty spaces around for weeds to fill up. Make it difficult for weeds to get established by planting spreading herbs such as mint, prostrate thyme, gotu kola and nasturtium.

If you've got an area that has become thick with perennial weeds, solarising or tarping the area in summer can be a good idea. Cut the weeds down to the ground, then cover them with a dark-coloured tarpaulin. Hold it in place with bricks or logs. Leave the tarp in place for a month or so and the weeds and their seeds will be cooked. Covering the cut-down weeds with thick layers of newspaper topped with mulch works well too.

Growing and using weeds

If you are interested in growing a particular weed in your garden, you may be able to source seeds from a neighbour or enthusiastic gardening friend. You can also keep a lookout on your travels around the neighbourhood. If you do head further afield to gather weeds, please note the following:

- make sure you are 100 per cent certain of what you are gathering
- check the area you are collecting them from hasn't been sprayed with chemical herbicides or exposed to pollutants like the side of a busy road
- only collect from plentiful populations – pick what you can use, leave some for wildlife regeneration and other foragers
- check that it's okay to be picking from the land you are on
- when you get home, give your foraged weeds a really good wash.

Here are some of my favourite medicinal herbs to grow and cook with:

- Chickweed (page 140)
- Cleavers (page 68)
- Dandelion (page 148)
- Elder (page 134)
- Hawthorn (page 44)
- Nettle (page 159)
- Plantain (page 118)

Weed tea

Make your own inexpensive liquid fertiliser by brewing up a bucket of weed tea. You can use the leaves and roots of almost any common weed or herb from the garden, but it's best to avoid using mature seed heads as this method may not make them inactive.

You will need
a bucket with a lid
a pot with a drainage hole to fit into the bucket
herbs or weeds from the garden

Fill the empty pot with weeds, then place the pot into a larger bucket that has no drainage holes.

Fill the bucket to the top with water, making sure all of the weeds are submerged. Pop the lid on to keep critters and rain out (and to keep the stink in!).

Place the bucket in a warm spot in the garden for 2–4 weeks.

When the weeds are sludgy, carefully take the pot out of the bucket, leaving the liquid behind. This can get pretty stinky, so wear gloves and old clothes.

The spent, sludgy plant material can go into the compost.

Use the liquid tea on your compost heap to speed up the decomposition, or as a nutrient-dense liquid fertiliser for your garden. When using, make a mixture of one part weed tea to ten parts water in a watering can, and apply to the soil around your plants.

Chapter 03
Harvesting and drying

Harvesting your herbs

Leaves and flowers

Leaves and flowers are best gathered during their growing season, usually spring and summer.

Head out to harvest leaves and flowers on a sunny morning, once the dew has dried off. If your plants are a little dusty, give them a clean up by gently spraying with the hose the day before you want to harvest.

Leaves high in aromatic oils are best harvested just before the plants are about to flower. Harvest flowers as they are just coming into full bloom, before they set seed.

Choose leaves and flowers that are fresh and vibrant, free from pest damage and disease. Snip herbs close to the base of the stem, just above a growth nodule, so the plant can spring forth another flush of growth. Pick flowers in bunches, or pick the flower heads individually.

Spread your herbal harvest out on a bench or table covered with a clean tablecloth or some newspaper. Pick through any damaged leaves, stray grasses and other plant material, stones, dirt and foreign objects – this is a process called garbling. The herbs are now ready to process into medicine, hang in bunches or place on screens to dry for use at a later date.

When harvesting flowers from a herb that you'll use berries from, such as elderflower, make sure to leave some flowers on the bush to turn into berries. No flowers; no berries.

Seeds

Harvest seeds just as they turn from green to brown. Cut the seed heads into a paper bag and leave them in a warm, dry spot until completely dry – the seeds will fall from the seed head into the bottom of the bag for easy collection.

Berries

Harvest berries when they are ripe, usually in mid- to late summer. Have a nibble on one to taste if it's ripe enough. Avoid harvesting green berries. Herbs such as rosehips are best harvested after the first frost; this gives them a sweeter taste.

Roots

Roots will need at least 1 year of growth before harvesting, with most herbs needing 2–3 years of root growth before you get a worthwhile harvest.

Harvest roots in late autumn or early spring, when the plant still has most of its stored energy in the root system.

Give the ground a good water a few days before you plan to harvest the roots. Trim down any aerial parts of the plant, leaving a few if you plan to divide the roots up for harvest and replanting. Use a garden fork and your hands to gently loosen the roots out of the ground. Shake loose dirt from the roots and give them a quick spray with a garden hose.

Scrub the roots thoroughly with a small scrubbing brush or an old toothbrush to get into all the little nooks and crannies. If the roots are twisted together, cut them apart so you can get all the dirt off. After they've been scrubbed, give the roots another rinse and dry them with a tea towel (dish towel).

Grate or chop the roots into smaller pieces while the root is fresh – they can be really tough and hard once dried. The roots are now ready to be processed into medicine or placed on screens to dry for use at a later date.

To maintain the life of your plant, harvest two-thirds of the roots and leave the rest to replant back into your garden bed. Give the garden bed a little refresh, working over with some compost and pulling out any weeds. Plant the roots back in the garden bed with the stems and shoots pointing upward. Water in, feed with some compost tea or weed tea, and mulch around the crown.

Drying your herbs

Choose a place to dry your herbs that is warm, dry and has good air circulation. It needs to be free of dust, smoke, insects and disruption from pets. Full sun, direct light and moisture are the enemies of your dried herbs. Try a walk in-pantry, closet or linen cupboard; a spot in the kitchen away from cooking smells and steam; a warm spot above the fridge; or the veranda in summer.

Hanging in bunches

Hanging bunches of herbs is not only a practical way of drying them, but also pretty. If you don't have much space in your home for a dehydrator or drying rack, hanging in bunches could be a good way to go. Bunching up herbs works best for those that have long stems such as yarrow and lavender. Culinary herbs also work well in small bunches.

Remove the lower leaves from the stem, and gather 5–10 stems to make a bunch. Don't overfill the bunches – they need good air circulation around the leaves and flowers. The middle can end up staying moist in humid or damp conditions and turn mouldy. Save up rubber bands from market-bought vegetables to tie bunches together. When the herbs dry, they shrink down. If you use string and forget to keep tightening them, the stems can fall out of the bunch. Placing a paper bag over the herbs can help reduce the humidity, protect the herbs from dust and light, and catch seeds if you're drying a seed head.

Hang the herb bunches upside down from a coat hanger or a piece of wooden dowel and check on them every few days for dryness.

Oven	Drying rack
Make use of the heat from your oven after cooking dinner or a day of baking. Alternatively, turn your oven to the lowest temperature possible, keep the door slightly ajar with a wooden spoon and place a tray of herbs inside. It can be hard to get an even temperature in the oven and even the lowest temperature may be too high for delicate blooms. To test out if your herbal leaves and flowers are dry, grab a few in your hand. They should feel papery crisp, and crumble into pieces if you crush them. Dried roots will have turned a darker colour and wrinkled up like a sultana. They should cleanly snap rather than bend when you try to break them in half. Cut them in half to check if the middle is dry. Leaves, flowers and roots will all feel much lighter than when they are fresh.	Racks and screens are a great use of passive energy and best to use in warm and dry conditions. You can find ready-made drying racks online, but you can easily repurpose household items. Baking trays lined with tissue paper or baking paper work well for larger leaves and flowers. Make use of old flyscreens, picture frames or canvas stretchers that you can staple fine mesh or netting onto. Stack the racks on top of each other making sure there is good circulation between them. Old bricks are good for this purpose. In winter, you can place the trays on a clothes-drying rack near the heater. In summer, keep the racks outside with an old net curtain on top to keep insects out and stop the herbs from blowing away. Place the herbs in a single layer, and turn regularly.

Dehydrator

Dehydrators are great if you live in an area where it's cold, damp or has high humidity, as there is an increased chance of mould and mildew spoiling your herbs in these conditions.

A dehydrator provides even temperature and dries herbs in a fairly quick time frame, which helps preserve the aromatics, colour and medicinal quality of the herbs. Make sure you use the lowest setting on your dehydrator for leaves and flowers, and medium for roots and berries. Most herbs like a drying temperature of 35–45°C (95°C–113°F).

Storing your herbs

Storing your herbs correctly is important, as herbs exposed to heat, direct light, air and moisture can lose their vibrant colour, aromatic oils and medicinal properties. Make sure your herbs have completely dried before placing them in airtight containers. Have a look in on them a few days after storing them. Check for condensation in the container and limp leaves or flowers. If they are still even the tiniest bit damp, remove them from the container and dry them for a while longer.

Remove woody stems from your dried herbs before storing. Keep leaves and flowers as whole as possible. Crush and powder up herbs as you need.

Store your dried herbs in airtight containers. Glass jars with tight fitting lids are the best. Keep the jars in a cool, dry, dark place like a kitchen pantry, cupboard or shelf that is out of direct light.

It's a good idea to label the jars with the date, the herb's name and the part harvested. You can easily forget what the herb is and many dried herbs look the same.

Dried leaves and flowers should last for 1–2 years and dried roots for 2–3 years.

Herbs that are past their prime may fade, or turn musty or moldy.

Chapter 04

Build your herbal medicine cabinet

The beauty of growing your own medicinal herb garden is that the possibilities for various recipes and remedies are endless. Create your own remedies for natural healing using these staple guides for making everything a budding natural medicine maker requires. Here are a few apothecary basics to get you started.

Teas and infusions

Herbal infusions are simple preparations that involve steeping herbs in water to extract their scent, flavour, colour and medicinal components. Despite their simplicity, herbal infusions can be powerful medicines with potent healing effects for our body and mind.

Herbal infusions are not just for drinking. Use as a soothing wash on a sunburn, a compress for sore and tired muscles and add to baths and foot soaks. You can choose your herbs based purely on scent, or you can choose herbs specifically for easing ailments such as tension headaches, cold and flu symptoms or an upset stomach. You can use fresh or dried herbs, add in citrus, berries and spices, and even sweeten with a spoonful of herbal honey.

DOSE

1–2 cups per day, for health giving properties.

2–6 cups per day, in the acute stages of illness.

Notes
Store unused tea in the fridge and use within 24 hours.

If you're using fresh herbs, double the measurement of dried herbs.

Garden tea

Makes 4 cups (Serves 4)

Once you have your potted tea garden up and growing, making a cup of tea is as simple as heading outside and finding inspiration amongst what is currently growing, blooming and fruiting.

Bring water to a boil in a medium saucepan or kettle.

While the water boils, roughly chop the herbs and place them in a 4-cup teapot.

Pour the boiling water over the herbs, place the lid on the teapot and let it all steep together for about 10 minutes. You should notice the water take on the colour of the herbs.

Gather four of your favourite teacups and pop a slice of lemon in each cup, along with a sprinkle of calendula petals.

Strain the tea into your prepared cups and compost the spent herbs.

Stir in a spoonful of honey into each cup if you'd like a sweeter brew.

Store unused tea in the fridge and use within 24 hours.

4 cups filtered water

1 cup fresh mixed herb leaves or ½ cup dried herbs

2 calendula flowers, petals removed from the sepal

4 lemon slices

raw honey, to taste (use local if available)

Herbal steam inhalation

The warm moist air from steam inhalations helps loosen mucus congestion in your head and lungs, as well as soothing the irritated linings of your nasal and airway passages. The addition of salt also reduces inflammation.

Gentle herbal steam

Aromatic herbs are the best for herbal steams, but you can use whatever you have on hand. Fresh bunches of thyme, sage leaves, sprigs of rosemary and lavender flowers are perfect, as well as dried herbs, cloves, cinnamon and ginger from the pantry. Basil, bee balm, chamomile, cinnamon, citrus rind, clove, eucalyptus, ginger, mullein, oregano, peppermint and yarrow are also great options.

Lightly crush the fresh herbs using a mortar and pestle or the back of a knife and add to a large bowl. If you are using dried herbs, place herbs straight into the bowl. Add the salt and cover with boiling water. Pop a dinner plate or lid over your bowl and let the herbs steep for 5–10 minutes.

Remove the lid from the bowl and make a 'steam tent' with a towel over your head and the bowl. Position your head about 20–30 cm above the bowl.

Close your eyes and start by trying long slow breaths through your nose and out through your mouth, eventually switching to just in and out through your nose to really clear up your head. Take breaks and blow your nose as needed. If you are feeling like things are too hot, move your head further away or remove the towel and take a break.

Each steam should last for about 10–15 minutes at the most, and you can repeat 2–3 times per day. To reheat, pop the herbs and water in a saucepan, cover with a lid and bring to a boil. Remove from the heat and pour the water and herbs back into your bowl and repeat the steaming process. If need be, you can freshen things up with a few extra springs of fresh herbs.

You will need
large bowl
large towel
tissues or a hanky

Ingredients
2 cups fresh herbs or 1 cup dried herbs
3–4 tablespoons salt
boiling water

Herbal posy

A herbal posy can be a mindful gift for a friend or a self-care treat for yourself. Gather herbs that you are naturally drawn to or those that are in seasonal abundance in your garden. You can also create posies specific to certain ailments such as headaches, an upset stomach or even cold and flu symptoms. Bunch the herbs together and secure with some string, place them in jars around your home, and use when showering or bathing by hanging them from the showerhead or tap.

UPSET TUMMY POSY

- Lemon balm
- Peppermint
- Catnip
- Fennel fronds
- Anise hyssop

HEADACHE POSY

- Lemon Balm
- Rosemary
- Gotu kola
- Feverfew
- Catnip
- Chamomile
- Peppermint

SLEEP POSY

- Lavender
- Lemon balm
- Chamomile
- Catnip
- Wood betony

COLD & FLU POSY

- Yarrow
- Peppermint
- Sage
- Thyme
- Oregano
- Echinacea
- Bee balm

Baths

Adding herbs and flowers to your bath can be an easy, relaxing way to reset and unwind. Here are a few ways to get the healing power of herbs into your bath that avoid leaving you and your tub covered in herbs post soak. The variations of herbs that you can add into your bath are endless. Popular bath herbs include chamomile, lavender, lemon balm, rosemary, mint, calendula and rose.

Add to the benefit of your bath by dry brushing with a Luffa massage brush beforehand (see page 90), or by adding skin-soothing extras such as coconut milk powder, Epsom salts or magnesium flakes.

Herbal bath infusion

Add a handful of your favourite herbs to a medium saucepan and cover with water. Bring the water to a boil, infusing the herbs for 10–15 minutes.

Once infused, pour the saucepan contents through a strainer or sieve into your bath. Add water to your bath as normal until you reach your desired temperature.

Herbal bath teabag

Bath teabags are great to hang over the tap while filling the bath or to have floating around in the water as you soak.

You can purchase re-usable tea bags for this, or try using a muslin cloth tied off with some ribbon or elastic. Simply fill up the teabag with your favourite herbs, tie it off and add to your bath.

Herbal bath salt soak

Makes enough for 6 baths

Combine your favourite medicinal herbs with some salt, oats and coconut milk powder in a blender or coffee grinder for a relaxing soak.

Combine all ingredients and blitz together in a coffee grinder or blender. You want the herbs to be as powder-like as possible to avoid large chunks or herbs in your bath.

Add ½ cup of your bath soak mixture directly under running water into your bath, mixing it in with your hand if needed. Soak for about 20–30 minutes, rinsing off afterwards. Keep bath mix in sealed container, label with date and ingredients.

1 cup Epsom salts
1 cup chunky rock salt
1 cup oats
1 cup coconut milk powder
½ cup arrowroot powder
1 tablespoon baking soda
2 cups medicinal herbs, any variety (chamomile and calendula are a personal favourite)

Foot soak

If you don't have a bath, foot soaks are a great alternative.

To make a foot soak, brew up and strain your herbs like you would for a bath.

Fill up a foot sized bucket, basin or pot with the herbal infusion, adding in cold water until it reaches your desired temperature. Soak your feet for about 10–15 minutes, adding more hot water as needed. If a foot massage sounds like something you could do with, pop a tennis ball or a sock filled with marbles into the foot bath to run your feet over.

Try the Peppermint foot soak for sore and tired feet (page 101).

Wash

Washes are herbal infusions (page 196) or diluted tinctures (page 203) that are used externally for a variety of conditions such as sunburn, rashes, grazes and cuts.

To make a wash, brew up a cup of medicinal herb infusion, or dilute 2 teaspoons of tincture in a cup of water. Dip in a flannel or cotton wool ball, squeeze out the excess liquid and gently wipe over the affected area.

Your wash can be warm or cold, depending on what you're using it for. Some lovely herbal combinations are chamomile and green tea for sunburn, and calendula and chickweed for rashes and grazes.

Compress

Compresses are similar to a wash, but a compress involves leaving the soaked cloth on the affected area for a longer time. Compresses are great for providing relief for headaches, burns, bruises, bites, sore throats, muscle tension, sprains and strains. My favourite herbs to use are chamomile, lemon balm, ginger, sage, lavender and calendula.

To make a compress use a flannel or piece of gauze and soak it in your herbal infusion (page 196). Squeeze out the excess, place it over the affected area and leave for about 10 minutes, resoaking and repeating as needed.

If you are using a cold infusion, replace the compress when it warms up. If you are using a warm infusion, potentiate the warmth by placing a heat pack or covered hot water bottle over the area.

Poultice

A poultice is an easy way to apply the medicinal properties of herbs directly to an affected area. A poultice can be made by simply crushing up herbs and placing on the affected area, or by covering a piece of cloth with a herb paste and placing on your body. Poultices are useful for drawing out stings, splinters and infections, speeding up the healing of sprains, strains and breaks and providing relief for painful skin conditions.

Herbal poultice

Blend the herbs and water in a blender until combined into a rough puree. Pour the blitzed herbs into a bowl and mix in small amounts of flour until it becomes a paste-like consistency.

Lay out one square of cloth on a cutting board. Place a spoonful of the herb mixture into the middle of the cloth. Spread the mixture out flat across the cloth, and lay a second piece of cloth over the top.

Place the poultice on the affected area. Keep on the area for at least 20 minutes. Secure in place with a bandage if need be. Repeat several times throughout the day.

Store your remaining poultice bundles in the freezer, layered between baking paper. You can then use the frozen poultice as you would an icepack.

See Comfrey leaf poultice (page 143), Onion poultice (page 19) and Quick lavender eye pillow (page 82).

- A bunch of fresh herbs (if using dried, rehydrate by soaking with some boiling water before straining)
- 1 cup water
- ¼ cup flour or cornflour
- 10 cm (4 inch) squares of gauze or cotton cloth, such as old sheets (relative to size of affected area)

Tincture

Besides herbal tea, tinctures are one of the most popular forms of herbal medicine. Tinctures include alcohol which is used as a solvent to draw out the medicinal properties of the herb. Tinctures are a quick and effective medicine as they are easily absorbed by our body through the blood stream. For home tincture making you can use the 'folk' method, which is simple to do and requires very few ingredients.

For the folk method, use a neutral spirit like vodka. It doesn't overpower the taste of the herb, which can be an important part of the herbs medicinal action. Choose a vodka that is at least 80 proof or higher.

herbs, fresh or dried
alcohol, 80–100 proof (40–50 per cent ABV)
sharp knife or scissors
mortar and pestle
glass jar with lid
butter knife or chopstick
baking paper
muslin cloth
fine metal sieve
glass measuring jug
funnel
amber glass bottles with lids

Chop the fresh herbs as finely as possible. Crush and crumble up dried herbs with your hands, or use a mortar and pestle to grind up harder herbs like dried roots, bark and seeds.

Fill a clean glass jar with the herbs (see the chart below for ratios). Top the jar up with the alcohol, making sure you cover the herbs by about an inch. Make sure the herbs are completely covered, as any air exposure could potentially cause mould to form.

Stir the contents with the blade of a butter knife or chopstick, pushing out any air bubbles and making sure there are no pockets of dried herbs. Top up with more alcohol if needed.

Place a lid on the jar. If you're using a metal lid, pop a piece of baking paper between the lid and jar to stop any potential corrosion. Give the jar another good shake before labelling and storing in a cool, dark place for 4–6 weeks.

For the first week, give the jar a shake every day or two and top up with more alcohol if needed.

When the tincture is ready, strain through a fine sieve lined with a muslin cloth into a large glass measuring jug. Gather the edges of the cloth around the herbs, and tightly squeeze out any excess liquid. If you have a potato ricer, these work really well to squeeze out every last drop. Compost the spent herbs.

Continues →

Decant the strained tincture through a funnel into clean, dark amber glass bottles. Pop a lid on the bottles and label with the date, herb name, herb part and solvent used. Store in a cool, dark place like a pantry or cupboard.

Take your tincture diluted in some water or juice. You can use hot water or herbal tea to evaporate some of the alcohol.

Tinctures are well preserved and shelf stable. Use within two years.

Herb parts & ratios

Fresh leaves and flowers: ¾ to full jar

Dried leaves and flowers: ½ to ¾ full

Fresh roots, berries and bark: ½ full

Dried roots, berries and bark: ¼ full

Herbal mouthwash

This tasty mouthwash is great for sensitive and bleeding gums. Use the tincture method in the previous recipe as a base for this mouthwash.

Using the thyme, calendula, yarrow, peppermint and alcohol, make the tincture according to the 'folk' method instructions.

Add 2 teaspoons of your tincture and salt into a glass with the warm water. Stir together.

To use your mouthwash, after brushing, swish a mouthful of wash gently in your mouth and through your teeth for 30 seconds. Gargle, then spit out. Rinse your mouth with plain water.

Use after brushing your teeth in the morning and evening. Decant and mix up a new batch for each day.

Tincture
1 tablespoon thyme
¼ cup calendula, whole flowers
¼ cup yarrow, leaves and flowers
¼ cup peppermint leaves
vodka

Mouthwash
2 teaspoons prepared tincture
¼ teaspoon salt
¼ cup warm water

Sprays

A spray is a great remedy to have on hand when you feel a sore throat coming on. This cold spray will feel cool and soothing on a hot, irritated throat.

Sore throat spray

Place the herbs, grated ginger and lemon rind into a small saucepan. Add a cup of water and bring to a boil. Pop a lid on and reduce the heat, simmering for 20 minutes. Turn off the heat and leave to steep overnight.

The next day, strain the herbs through a fine sieve, using the back of a spoon to extract maximum liquid. Stir in the honey and alcohol and pour into a clean, sterilised spray bottle.

Store spray in the fridge for up to 6 months.

DOSAGE

For adults use 4–5 sprays, every 2–3 hours as needed.

- 2 tablespoons dried thyme
- 2 tablespoons dried sage
- 2 tablespoons dried echinacea leaf, flower and root
- 2 tablespoons dried marshmallow root
- Rind of ½ a lemon
- 1 inch piece of ginger
- ¾ cup vodka or brandy (at least 40 per cent ABV)
- 3 tablespoons raw honey

Chapter 05
Herbal charts

COMMON NAME	PART USED	PREPARATION	BODY PART/SYSTEM	CAUTIONS
YARROW	flower, leaf	compress, food, tea, tincture, wash	digestive, respiratory, skin	known allergen
ANISE HYSSOP	flower, leaf	compress, food, steam inhalation, tea, tincture, wash	digestive, nervous, respiratory, skin	
ONION	bulb	food, poultice	cardiovascular, digestive, respiratory	known allergen; avoid using alongside anticoagulant and antiplatelet drugs
GARLIC	bulb	food, honey, infused oil, tincture	cardiovascular, digestive, respiratory	known allergen; avoid using alongside anticoagulant and antiplatelet drugs
ALOE	gel, leaf	food, topical application	digestive, skin	avoid internal use during pregnancy and lactation; use only for short periods of time
MARSHMALLOW	flower, leaf, root	compress, food, tea, tincture, wash	digestive, respiratory, skin, urinary	may reduce absorption of prescribed drugs if taken within an hour or so of each other
HORSERADISH	flower, leaf, root	food, poultice, tincture	musculoskeletal, respiratory	avoid in high doses in peptic ulcers, pregnancy, hypothyroidism
WOOD BETONY	flower, leaf	compress, food, tea, tincture, wash	nervous	
CALENDULA	flower	compress, food, tea, tincture, wash	lymphatic, skin	known allergen
GOTU KOLA	leaf	compress, food, tea, tincture, wash	cardiovascular, nervous, skin	known allergen
HAWTHORN	berry, flower, leaf	food, tea, tincture	cardiovascular	avoid if using beta-blockers, digitalis-based drugs, heart medications

COMMON NAME	PART USED	PREPARATION	BODY PART/SYSTEM	CAUTIONS
TURMERIC	rhizome	food, poultice, tea, tincture	digestive, musculoskeletal, skin	taking anti-platelet drugs
GLOBE ARTICHOKE	leaf	food, tea, tincture	digestive	known allergen
ECHINACEA	flower, leaf, root	compress, food, tincture, wash	immune, lymphatic, respiratory, skin	known allergen
CALIFORNIA POPPY	flower, leaf, root, seed	food, tea, tincture	nervous	avoid during pregnancy and if taking MAOIs (monoamine oxidase inhibitor)
MEADOWSWEET	flower	food, tea, tincture	digestive, nervous, respiratory	salicylate (aspirin) sensitivity, taking warfarin
FENNEL	flower, leaf	food, tea, tincture	digestive, lactation, respiratory	gastro-oesophageal reflux
CLEAVERS	leaf, seed	compress, food, tea, tincture, wash	lymphatic, skin, urinary	known allergen
LICORICE	root	compress, food, tea, tincture, wash	digestive, respiratory, skin	avoid long time use of high doses, during pregnancy, lactation, hypertension, hypokalaemia, oedema, congestive heart failure, heart, liver or kidney disease and alongside laxative use
HOPS	flower	food, tea, tincture	nervous	depression, oestrogen-sensitive
LAVENDER	flower	compress, food, poultice, steam inhalation, tea, tincture, wash	digestive, nervous, skin	known allergen

COMMON NAME	PART USED	PREPARATION	BODY PART/SYSTEM	CAUTIONS
MOTHERWORT	flower, leaf	food, tea, tincture	cardiovascular, nervous, reproductive	heavy menstrual bleeding, pregnancy
LUFFA	fruit	food, sponge	lymphatic, musculoskeletal	
CHAMOMILE	flower	compress, food, tea, tincture, wash	digestive, nervous, skin	known allergen
LEMON BALM	flower, leaf	compress, food, tea, tincture, wash	digestive, nervous, skin	
PEPPERMINT	flower, leaf	food, tea, tincture, wash	digestive, respiratory, skin	gastro-oesophageal reflux; avoid contact with undiluted essential oil on sensitive skin
BERGAMOT	flower, leaf	compress, food, steam inhalation, tea, tincture, wash	digestive, nervous, respiratory, skin	avoid medicinal use during pregnancy
CATNIP	flower, leaf	food, steam inhalation, tea, tincture	digestive, nervous, respiratory	avoid during pregnancy
TULSI	flower, leaf	food, steam inhalation, tea, tincture	cardiovascular, digestive, immune, nervous, respiratory, skin	
OREGANO	flower, leaf	compress, food, tea, tincture, wash	digestive, respiratory	known allergen, avoid contact with undiluted essential oil on sensitive skin
PARSLEY	flower, leaf, root	food, tea, tincture	digestive, reproductive, urinary	avoid during pregnancy and breastfeeding
PLANTAIN	leaf, seed	food, poultice, tea, tincture, wash	digestive, respiratory, skin	known allergen

COMMON NAME	PART USED	PREPARATION	BODY PART/SYSTEM	CAUTIONS
ROSE	flower, hips	food, steam inhalation, tea, tincture, wash	cardiovascular, nervous, skin	
SAGE	flower, leaf	compress, food, steam inhalation, tea, tincture, wash	digestive, reproductive, respiratory	avoid contact with undiluted essential oil on sensitive skin
ROSEMARY	flower, leaf	food, steam inhalation, tea, tincture, wash	digestive, musculoskeletal, respiratory, skin	avoid contact with undiluted essential oil on sensitive skin
ELDER	berry, flower, leaf (external use only)	food, tea, tincture, wash	immune, respiratory, skin	avoid green and raw berries; internal use of leaf may cause nausea and vomiting
SKULLCAP	flower, leaf	food, tea, tincture	digestive, nervous, reproductive	
CHICKWEED	flower, leaf	compress, food, tincture, wash	digestive, skin	known allergen
COMFREY	leaf, root	compress, poultice	musculoskeletal	external preparations only
FEVERFEW	flower, leaf	food, tea, tincture, wash	digestive, musculoskeletal, nervous	avoid during pregnancy
DANDELION	flower, leaf, root	food, tea, tincture	digestive, liver, skin, urinary	known allergen; gall bladder disease, gallstones
THYME	flower, leaf	food, steam inhalation, tea, tincture, wash	digestive, respiratory	known allergen, avoid contact with undiluted essential oil on sensitive skin
NASTURTIUM	flower, leaf, seed pod	compress, food, tincture, wash	digestive, respiratory, skin, urinary	avoid with peptic ulcer

COMMON NAME	PART USED	PREPARATION	BODY PART/SYSTEM	CAUTIONS
NETTLE	leaf, root, seed	compress, food, tea, tincture, wash	musculoskeletal, respiratory, skin, urinary	known allergen; avoid contact with skin, overconsumption may cause urticaria (itchy skin)
VALERIAN	flower, root	food, tea, tincture	musculoskeletal, nervous	may have stimulant or excitatory effect for some
MULLEIN	flower, leaf, root	food, infused oil, steam inhalation, tea, tincture	musculoskeletal, respiratory	
VIOLET	flower, leaf	food, tea, tincture, wash	lymphatic, respiratory, skin	
GINGER	rhizome	compress, food, tea, tincture	circulatory, digestive, musculoskeletal, respiratory	gallstones, peptic ulcer, pregnancy, taking warfarin

Herbal charts

Index

Note: **Bolded** entries indicate plants that have individual profiles within the book.

A

agave, nectar: Aloe vera popsicles 25
alcohol *see also* Tincture
    Bergamot and blood orange granita 105
    Echinacea, ginger and thyme syrup 57
    Sore throat spray 205
    Herbal mouthwash 204
aloe vera 22, 207
    Aloe vera popsicles 25
anise hyssop 15, 207
    Summer berry ice cream with anise 16
    upset tummy posy 198
apples: Spiced hawthorn and apple fruit leather 47
artichoke, globe 52, 208
avocadoes: Garden greens dip 171

B

bananas: Chocolate and tulsi nice cream 110
baths 199
    Herbal bath salt soak 199
    herbal bath teabag 199
beans: Garden greens dip 171
bed preparation 178
bee balm: cold & flu posy 198
Beetroot, berry and betony salad 35
bergamot 102–3, 209
    Bergamot and blood orange granita 105
betony, wood 32, 207
    Beetroot, berry and betony salad 35
    sleep posy 198
biscuits, Calendula butter 39
    Bittersweet chocolate truffles 86
blackberries
    Beetroot, berry and betony salad 35
    blackberry jam vinaigrette 35
    Summer berry ice cream with anise 16
blueberries: Beetroot, berry and betony salad 35
broth, Medicinal bone 117
butter, Herb, with feverfew 147

C

cakes
    Lemon and nettle cake with elderberry cream cheese icing 160–1
    Mandarin and rosemary cake 132
calendula 36, 207
    Aloe vera popsicles 25
    Calendula butter biscuits 39
    Feverfew and spring greens frittata 146
    Garden tea 196
    Herbal bath salt soak 199
    Herbal mouthwash 204
    Medicinal bone broth 117
    Mullein and garlic ear oil 168
    Wild weed pie 151
California poppy *see* poppy, California
capers: Oregano salsa verde 113
carrots
    Gotu kola salad 42
    Medicinal bone broth 117
catnip 106, 209
    Aloe vera popsicles 25
    headache posy 198
    sleep posy 198
    upset tummy posy 198
cauliflower: Spicy cauliflower bites 51
celery: Medicinal bone broth 117
chamomile 93, 182, 209
    Chamomile, thyme and honey panna cotta 94
    compress 201
    headache posy 198
    Herbal bath salt soak 199
    sleep posy 198
chard, rainbow: Feverfew and spring greens frittata 146
cheese
    Beetroot, berry and betony salad 35
    Chickweed pesto 141
    elderberry cream cheese icing 160
    Feverfew and spring greens frittata 146
    Lemon and nettle cake with elderberry cream cheese icing 160–1
    Wild weed pie 151
chicken: Medicinal bone broth 117

chickweed 140, 210
    Chickweed pesto 141
    Feverfew and spring greens frittata 146
    Garden greens dip 171
chilli
    Gotu kola salad 42
    Spicy cauliflower bites 51
chives: Feverfew and spring greens frittata 146
chocolate
    Bittersweet chocolate truffles 86
    Chocolate and tulsi nice cream 110
    Nettle seed bites 161
    Nourish fennel cookies 67
    Valerian spiced hot chocolate 165
cleavers 68, 208
    Cleavers coffee 71
coconut
    Aloe vera popsicles 25
    Bittersweet chocolate truffles 86
    Chocolate and tulsi nice cream 110
    Gotu kola salad 42
    Herbal bath salt soak 199
    Nettle seed bites 161
    Rose, hibiscus and vanilla marshmallows 28–9
coffee, Cleavers 71
cold & flu posy 198
comfrey 142, 182, 210
    Comfrey leaf poultice 143
compost 179
compress 201
cookies, Nourish fennel 67
crackers, Plantain seed 121
crumble, Meadowsweet and rhubarb, with meadowsweet custard 63
cucumbers: Aloe vera popsicles 25
custard, meadowsweet 63

D

dandelion 148, 182, 210
    Feverfew and spring greens frittata 146
    Garden greens dip 171
    Medicinal bone broth 117
    Wild weed pie 151
dates: Chocolate and tulsi nice cream 110
deodorant, Sage 128
dip, Garden greens 171

dressings 99
    blackberry jam vinaigrette 35
    yoghurt dressing 99

E
ear oil, Mullein and garlic 168
echinacea 54, 208
    cold & flu posy 198
    Echinacea, ginger and thyme syrup 57
    Sore throat spray 205
eggs
    Feverfew and spring greens frittata 146
    Meadowsweet and rhubarb crumble with meadowsweet custard 63
    meadowsweet custard 63
    Summer berry ice cream with anise 16
elder 134, 210
    elderberry cream cheese icing 160
    Elderberry gummies 136
    Elderflower fritters 137
    Lemon and nettle cake with elderberry cream cheese icing 160–1
    Spiced elderberry syrup 135
    Summer berry ice cream with anise 16
eye pillow, Quick lavender 82

F
face mask, Rose and oat 125
fennel 64, 208
    Feverfew and spring greens frittata 146
    Nourish fennel cookies 67
    upset tummy posy 198
    Wild weed pie 151
Fermented garlic honey 21
feverfew 144, 210
    Feverfew and spring greens frittata 146
    headache posy 198
    Herb butter with feverfew 147
foot soak 200
foot soak, Peppermint 101
frittata, Feverfew and spring greens 146
fritters, Elderflower 137
fritters, Lemon balm, pea and zucchini 99
fruit leather, Spiced hawthorn and apple 47

G
Garden greens dip 171
Garden tea 196
gardening
    bed preparation 178
    compost 179
    growing a potted tea garden 181
    growing and using weeds 184
    harvesting herbs 188–9
    herbs for garden care 182–3
    herbs in containers 180–1
    making a lasagne bed 178
    mulch 179
    weeds 184
garlic 20, 207
    Chickweed pesto 141
    Fermented garlic honey 21
    Garden greens dip 171
    Herb butter with feverfew 147
    Hops shoot pickles 78
    Lemon balm, pea and zucchini fritters 99
    Medicinal bone broth 117
    Mullein and garlic ear oil 168
    Oregano salsa verde 113
    Pod pickles 156
    Wild weed pie 151
Gentle herbal steam 197
ginger 172, 211
    compress 201
    Echinacea, ginger and thyme syrup 57
    Elderberry gummies 136
    Ginger and lemongrass lozenges 175
    Nettle seed bites 161
    Sore throat spray 205
    Spiced elderberry syrup 135
    Valerian spiced hot chocolate 165
globe artichoke 52, 208
gotu kola 41, 207
    Garden greens dip 171
    Gotu kola salad 42
    headache posy 198
growing medicinal plants 178–9
gummies, Elderberry 136

H
hawthorn 44, 207
    Spiced hawthorn and apple fruit leather 47
headache posy 198
Herb butter with feverfew 147
herbal bath infusion 199
Herbal bath salt soak 199
herbal bath teabag 199

Herbal mouthwash 204
herbal posy 198
Herbal poultice 202
herbal steam inhalation 197
herbs
    drying 190–3
    foot soak 200
    for garden care 182–3
    Garden tea 196
    Gentle herbal steam 197
    growing a potted tea garden 181
    growing in containers 180
    harvesting 188–9
    herbal bath infusion 199
    Herbal bath salt soak 199
    herbal bath teabag 199
    herbal posy 198
    Herbal poultice 202
    storing 193
hibiscus: Rose, hibiscus and vanilla marshmallows 28–9
honey
    California poppy sweet dreams milk 61
    Chamomile, thyme and honey panna cotta 94
    Echinacea, ginger and thyme syrup 57
    Fermented garlic honey 21
    Ginger and lemongrass lozenges 175
    Meadowsweet and rhubarb crumble with meadowsweet custard 63
    Nettle seed bites 161
    Rose and oat face mask 125
    Rose, hibiscus and vanilla marshmallows 28–9
    Sore throat spray 205
    Valerian spiced hot chocolate 165
hops 77, 208
    Hops shoot pickles 78
horseradish 30, 207
hot chocolate, Valerian spiced 165

I
ice cream, Summer berry, with anise 16
icing, elderberry cream cheese 160
infusions 196
    herbal bath infusion 199

L

lasagne beds 178
lavender 81, 208
   compress 201
   Lavender lemonade scones 83
   Quick lavender eye pillow 82
   sleep posy 198
leeks: Wild weed pie 151
lemon
   Aloe vera popsicles 25
   Bergamot and blood orange granita 105
   Chickweed pesto 141
   Echinacea, ginger and thyme syrup 57
   elderberry cream cheese icing 160
   Elderflower fritters 137
   Garden tea 196
   Herb butter with feverfew 147
   Lavender lemonade scones 83
   Lemon and nettle cake with elderberry cream cheese icing 160–1
   Lemon balm, pea and zucchini fritters 99
   Meadowsweet and rhubarb crumble with meadowsweet custard 63
   Medicinal bone broth 117
   Oregano salsa verde 113
   Peppermint foot soak 101
   Sore throat spray 205
   Spiced elderberry syrup 135
   Wild rosehip syrup 124
   Wild weed pie 151
   yoghurt dressing 99
lemon balm 96, 209
   Aloe vera popsicles 25
   compress 201
   Feverfew and spring greens frittata 146
   Garden greens dip 171
   headache posy 198
   Lemon balm, pea and zucchini fritters 99
   sleep posy 198
   upset tummy posy 198
   yoghurt dressing 99
lemongrass: Ginger and lemongrass lozenges 175
licorice 72, 208
   Licorice logs 75
limes
   Aloe vera popsicles 25
   Garden greens dip 171
   Gotu kola salad 42
lozenges, Ginger and lemongrass 175

luffa 88, 209
   Luffa massage brush 90–1

M

mallow: Feverfew and spring greens frittata 146
Mandarin and rosemary cake 132
marshmallow 27, 207
   Rose, hibiscus and vanilla marshmallows 28–9
   Sore throat spray 205
massage brush, Luffa 90–1
meadowsweet 62, 208
   meadowsweet custard 63
   Meadowsweet and rhubarb crumble with meadowsweet custard 63
Medicinal bone broth 117
medicinal plants, growing 178–9
milk, California poppy sweet dreams 61
mint
   Aloe vera popsicles 25
   Beetroot, berry and betony salad 35
   Feverfew and spring greens frittata 146
   Garden greens dip 171
   Gotu kola salad 42
   Herb butter with feverfew 147
   Lemon balm, pea and zucchini fritters 99
   Oregano salsa verde 113
   Wild weed pie 151
motherwort 85, 209
   Bittersweet chocolate truffles 86
mouthwash, Herbal 204
mulch 179
mullein 167, 211
   Mullein and garlic ear oil 168

N

nasturtium 155, 210
   Pod pickles 156
nettle 159, 182, 211
   Feverfew and spring greens frittata 146
   Lemon and nettle cake with elderberry cream cheese icing 160–1
   Medicinal bone broth 117
   Nettle seed bites 161
nice cream, Chocolate and tulsi 110
Nourish fennel cookies 67

O

oats
   Herbal bath salt soak 199
   Nettle seed bites 161
   Nourish fennel cookies 67
   Rose and oat face mask 125
oil, Mullein and garlic ear 168
onion 18, 207
   Beetroot, berry and betony salad 35
   Gotu kola salad 42
   Medicinal bone broth 117
   Onion poultice 19
   Wild weed pie 151
orange
   Bergamot and blood orange granita 105
   Elderberry gummies 136
   Meadowsweet and rhubarb crumble with meadowsweet custard 63
   Spiced elderberry syrup 135
   Valerian spiced hot chocolate 165
oregano 112, 209
   cold & flu posy 198
   Medicinal bone broth 117
   Oregano salsa verde 113

P

panna cotta, Chamomile, thyme and honey 94
parsley 114, 209
   Beetroot, berry and betony salad 35
   Feverfew and spring greens frittata 146
   Garden greens dip 171
   Gotu kola salad 42
   Herb butter with feverfew 147
   Medicinal bone broth 117
   Oregano salsa verde 113
peas: Lemon balm, pea and zucchini fritters 99
peppermint 100, 209
   cold & flu posy 198
   Ginger and lemongrass lozenges 175
   headache posy 198
   Herbal mouthwash 204
   Peppermint foot soak 101
   upset tummy posy 198
pesto, Chickweed 141
pickles
   Hops shoot pickles 78
   Pod pickles 156
pie, Wild weed 151

plantain 118, 209
    Plantain seed crackers 121
Pod pickles 156
poppy, California 58, 208
    California poppy sweet dreams milk 61
popsicles, Aloe vera 25
posy, herbal 198
pots, growing herbs in 180
poultice 202
    Comfrey leaf poultice 143
    Herbal poultice 202
    Onion poultice 19

Q

Quick lavender eye pillow 82

R

rhubarb: Meadowsweet and rhubarb crumble with meadowsweet custard 63
rose 122, 210
    Bittersweet chocolate truffles 86
    California poppy sweet dreams milk 61
    Mandarin and rosemary cake 132
    Rose and oat face mask 125
    Rose, hibiscus and vanilla marshmallows 28–9
    Spiced hawthorn and apple fruit leather 47
    Wild rosehip syrup 124
rosemary 131, 210
    headache posy 198
    Mandarin and rosemary cake 132
    Peppermint foot soak 101
    Plantain seed crackers 121
    Sage deodorant 128

S

sage 127, 210
    cold & flu posy 198
    compress 201
    Medicinal bone broth 117
    Sage deodorant 128
    Sore throat spray 205
salads
    Beetroot, berry and betony salad 35
    Gotu kola salad 42
salsa verde, Oregano 113
salt soak, Herbal bath 199
sauce: Oregano salsa verde 113
scones, Lavender lemonade 83

skullcap 139, 210
sleep posy 198
soak, foot 200
soak, Herbal bath salt 199
Sore throat spray 205
Spiced elderberry syrup 135
Spiced hawthorn and apple fruit leather 47
Spicy cauliflower bites 51
spinach: Feverfew and spring greens frittata 146
sprays 205
    Sore throat spray 205
steam, Gentle herbal 197
steam inhalation, herbal 197
Summer berry ice cream with anise 16
syrups
    Spiced elderberry syrup 135
    Wild rosehip syrup 124

T

teas 196
    Garden tea 196
    growing a potted tea garden 181
    herbal bath teabag 199
    Weed tea 185
throat spray, Sore 205
thyme 152, 210
    Chamomile, thyme and honey panna cotta 94
    cold & flu posy 198
    Echinacea, ginger and thyme syrup 57
    Herbal mouthwash 204
    Medicinal bone broth 117
    Sore throat spray 205
Tincture 203
tofu: Lemon balm, pea and zucchini fritters 99
truffles, Bittersweet chocolate 86
tulsi 109, 209
    California poppy sweet dreams milk 61
    Chocolate and tulsi nice cream 110
turmeric 48, 208
    Spicy cauliflower bites 51

U

upset tummy posy 198

V

valerian 162, 183, 211
    Valerian spiced hot chocolate 165

vinaigrette, blackberry jam 35
violet 170, 211
    Feverfew and spring greens frittata 146
    Garden greens dip 171

W

wash 200
Weed tea 185
weeds 184
    Chickweed 140
    Cleavers 68
    Dandelion 148
    Elder 134
    growing and using 184
    Hawthorn 44
    Plantain 118
    Nettle 159
    weed management 18
    Weed tea 185
    Wild weed pie 151
    Wild rosehip syrup 124
    Wild weed pie 151
wood betony see betony, wood

Y

yarrow 12, 183, 207
    cold & flu posy 198
    Herbal mouthwash 204
yoghurt
    dressing 99
    Rose and oat face mask 125

Z

zucchini: Lemon balm, pea and zucchini fritters 99

First published in Australia in 2024 by
Thames & Hudson Australia
Wurundjeri Country, 132A Gwynne Street,
Cremorne, Victoria 3121

First published in the United Kingdom in 2025 by
Thames & Hudson Ltd
6–24 Britannia Street, London WC1X 9JD

First published in the United States of America in 2025 by
Thames & Hudson Inc.
500 Fifth Avenue, New York, New York 10110

The Medicinal Garden © Thames & Hudson Australia 2024
The Healing Garden © Thames & Hudson Australia 2024

Text © Caroline Parker 2024
Illustrations © Lucy Mora 2024

27 26 25   5 4 3 2

The moral right of the author has been asserted.

All rights reserved. No part of this publication may be reproduced or transmitted in any form or by any means, electronic or mechanical, including photocopy, recording or any other information storage or retrieval system, without prior permission in writing from the publisher.

ISBN 978-1-760-76426-5
ISBN 978-1-760-76466-1 (U.S. edition)
ISBN 978-1-760-76496-8 (ebook)

EU Authorized Representative: Interart S.A.R.L.
19 rue Charles Auray, 93500 Pantin, Paris, France
productsafety@thameshudson.co.uk
www.interart.fr

 A catalogue record for this book is available from the National Library of Australia

British Library Cataloguing-in-Publication Data
A catalogue record for this book is available from the British Library

Library of Congress Control Number 2024935896

Front cover illustration: Lucy Mora

Design: Ashlea O'Neill | Salt Camp Studio
Series concept: Jo Turner
Editing: Martine Lleonart
Printed and bound in China by C&C Offset Printing Co., Ltd

Thames & Hudson Australia wishes to acknowledge that Aboriginal and Torres Strait Islander peoples are the first storytellers of this nation and the Traditional Custodians of the land on which we live and work. We acknowledge their continuing culture and pay respect to Elders past and present.

Be the first to know about our new releases, exclusive content and author events by visiting
thamesandhudson.com.au
thamesandhudson.com
thamesandhudsonusa.com

ACKNOWLEDGEMENTS

A massive thank you to the Lucys in my life. Lucy Mora for bringing the herbs and recipes in this book to life with your beautiful illustrations. And to Dr Lucy Nairn, my farm wife. Thank you for letting me get my hands in the dirt on the farm, for sharing so much with me these past few years, and for your firm words of support and encouragement.

Thank you to my herbie cheerleader Jessica Bosscha, as well as the rest of my wonderful friends, peers and mentors at Estuary Learning. Thank you to Lisa Worth for eating allll of the licorice.

Mum, Dad and Nicole. Playing and helping out in our many gardens are the strongest and fondest memories of my childhood.

Thanks to all my wonderful friends that have joined me on forest walks, winter swims, for cups of tea and for reading through pages and pages of my writing. Yvonne, my dearest friend and fellow plant nerd.

To all the gardeners, farmers, herbalists, teachers and plant lovers that have weaved through my life – online and in person – I am ever grateful for the inspiration, knowledge and wisdom shared with me, I promise to keep sharing it around.

Thank you to Kirsten Abbott, Shannon Grey and Martine Lleonart for lovingly bringing this book together.

Leon, your love and support got me here. Thank you for all the stealth plant cuttings. I love you.